The Vodafone Dictionary of

Cricket

Edited by Laurie Brannan

vodafone

First published in Great Britain 2003
by Sportsguide Press
Telstar House
High Street
Crowthorne
Berkshire
RG45 7AT
info@sportsguidelimited.com

ISBN 0 95447100 8

Dictionary of Cricket A–Z © Laurie Brannan 2003.

Official Laws of Cricket © Marylebone Cricket Club 1980, 1988, 1992, 2000.

Front cover photograph courtesy of PA Photos.

Printed and bound in Great Britain by Creative Print and Design, Ebbw Vale.
Designed and typeset by John Berry, john_berry@hotmail.com.

Contents

Foreword

by **Lord MacLaurin**

'Cricket is first and foremost a dramatic spectacle,' wrote the great Trinidadian cricket writer C.L.R. James. 'It belongs with the theatre, ballet, opera and the dance.'

Every true cricket fan will endorse that opinion, but the greatest drama draws its power from language, and it is the language of cricket which makes this sport so very distinctive – not only the familiar everyday lexicon of googlies, yorkers and maidens, but also the more exotic phraseology which is more rarely uttered, but none the less adds to the mystique and character of our great game. It is a mark of the impact of cricket on our national life that so many of its terms have entered and enriched the English language.

As a former Chairman of the England and Wales Cricket Board, I am delighted that *The Vodafone Dictionary of Cricket* has not only brought together all the weird and wonderful words and phrases which make up the language of the sport, but is also providing the most up-to-date version of the Laws.

This winning combination makes the book an essential companion for every cricketer at every level of the game, and as Chairman, I am proud of Vodafone's involvement with it.

Preface

by **Laurie Brannan**, editor

My sincere thanks are due to Vodafone, who commissioned this book, and in particular to its Group Corporate Affairs Director, Tim Brown, without whose vision this work would still be gathering dust on the shelf.

The bricks and mortar of the dictionary have been drawn from a variety of sources, and while it is impossible to acknowledge all those involved, it would be remiss of me not to mention a few whose contributions have been invaluable.

At the very top of this list is good friend and colleague, journalist Bill Day, whose passion for the game is incomparable. His skill in providing such succinct definitions to many of the words and phrases so painstakingly researched, initially by Rishi Persad and subsequently Jonathon Bates, has been indispensable in the development of the text.

I am also greatly indebted to the Marylebone Cricket Club for allowing the inclusion of the Laws of Cricket, for the constructive appraisal of their Chief Executive Roger Knight, and for the help and efficiency of his personal assistant Stephanie Lawrence in bringing the project to fruition.

The advice of various professionals and academics must be also be recognised – most notably television commentator and former England coach David Lloyd; Richard Lewis, ex-Hampshire player and now professional at Charterhouse; Peter Shilston, master in History and Political Philosophy at Wellington College; and journalists Alan Lee and Christopher Poole.

As with any living language, the vocabulary of cricket is constantly evolving, and my final thank you, therefore, goes in advance to those readers kind enough to advise me of possible entries for future editions.

Introduction

by **Ian Botham**

The game of cricket is as simple or as complicated as you want to make it.

At one level there are two kids on the beach with bat, ball and an improvised wicket. At another there are the tortured calculations of the Duckworth/Lewis method when rain interrupts a one-day match.

Between such extremes lies an international sport with a set of laws some of which seem all but impenetrable to outsiders, and with a colourful vocabulary all its own.

The aim of *The Vodafone Dictionary of Cricket* is a simple one – to enlighten those seeking a greater knowledge of the game by providing in the first part a comprehensive and easy-to-use alphabetical guide to its language, and in the second part the most up-to-date version of the Laws, together with diagrams of field placings.

The great majority of the cricketing terms in the dictionary section of the book are culled from the commentary box or the players' changing room, and I could tell you the exact derivation of plenty of them.

Buffet ball, for example – here defined as 'A ball so poorly delivered it encourages the batsman to help himself' – was certainly coined in the commentary box, and plenty of others have a familiar ring.

Many of the most memorable terms – *zooter*, for instance, or *moon shot* or *yahoo* – encapsulate that humour which is such an integral part of the game, and in general the peculiar language with which cricket is described and recorded provides a lasting expression of its unique quality, so perfectly expressed in 'The Spirit of Cricket' which forms the preamble to the Laws.

The Vodafone Dictionary of Cricket is your pass to the commentary box and the players' balcony. Welcome in!

The Vodafone Dictionary of

Cricket

vodafone

Edited by

Laurie Brannan

A

abandoned
Match called off, most commonly for bad weather.

account
Term used to describe a batsman's score.

across the line
Shot played by a batsman across the path of the approaching ball.

action (bowling)
The movement of a bowler's arms, shoulders, trunk and legs at the point of delivery. Also relates to how much spin or swing the bowler has imparted on the ball.

Adelaide Oval
Established in 1871, it is not only the longest but is considered to be the most picturesque of Australia's Test grounds, set in parklands with the backdrop of St Peter's Cathedral. Seating capacity: 25,000.

aggregate
Combined total of runs scored by a batsman in a competition series, a tour, a season of cricket. Also applies to a bowler's total of wickets taken in a given time.

agricultural shot
Batting stroke not found in a recognised coaching manual.

air
Bowler dispatches ball at a higher trajectory (as in giving the ball air).

air shot
Shot played by the striking batsman that does not make contact with the ball.

akara
Indian for an unprepared wicket.

alley
A metaphorical line just outside the off stump. *See* **corridor of uncertainty.**

all out
The end of a team's innings.

all-rounder
A player with specialist skills in two or more disciplines.

all-run four
Results when a batman's shot fails to reach to boundary, but the ball is not retrieved and returned by the fielder before the bastmen have run between the wickets four times.

all weather pitch
A wicket made from composite materials needing little maintenance and enabling play in adverse weather conditions.

amateur

Status of a non-paid player.

analysis

A bowler's figures at the end of an innings. It logs overs bowled, maiden overs, runs scored off deliveries and wickets taken. *See* **figures**.

anchor-man

A steady, calming, studied role performed by a batsman to shore up an innings.

angled bat

Shot employed by a batsman using the pace of the ball to deflect it behind square. *See* **square**.

ankler

A ball struck low with pace to a fielder.

anorak

Slightly derogatory description of an enthusiast with an insatiable appetite for knowledge of all aspects of the game. *See* **zealot**.

anticipation

Ability to pre-empt the line of the ball, particularly vital to batsmen and wicket keepers.

anti-corruption unit

Intelligence-gathering organisation working under the auspices of the International Cricket Council to police, monitor and frustrate inappropriate elements within the sport. *See* **International Cricket Coucil**.

Antigua Recreation Ground

The most recent addition to the West Indies' Test match venues, it is located in the Antiguan capital of St John's and, uniquely, the playing surface is maintained by inmates of the adjoining prison under the supervision of the warden.

apartheid

Political movement which discriminated against blacks and resulted in international teams boycotting South African cricket.

appeal

The fielding team's request to the umpire for a batsman to be given out.

apprentice

A player indentured to a club receiving tuition in lieu of payment.

Arbab Niaz Stadium

Northern Pakistan Test ground in Peshawar.

area of rough

A scuffed-up surface of the pitch, encouraging spin bowling.

arm ball

A delivery that continues its line after pitching. Also known as a floater.

arm guard

Protective cover to shield a batsman's forearm from a rising delivery. *See* **rising delivery**.

armoury

Usually a team's bowling line-up and the weapons at the captain's disposal.

around the wicket

The path taken by a right-arm bowler wanting to deliver the ball with the stumps on his left side at the point of release.

a-run-a-ball

The ratio at which a batsman or team score their runs during an innings.

Asgiriya Stadium

Sri Lankan Test match venue set in the grounds of Trinity College in Kandy and surrounded by hills which cast long shadows across the playing surface in the late afternoon.

Ashes, The

England were so humiliated by an Australian side at The Oval in August 1882 that the following mock obituary notice appeared in the *Sporting Times*: 'in affectionate remembrance of English cricket which died on The Oval, on August 29th, 1882. Deeply lamented by a large circle of sorrowing friends and acquaintances. R.I.P. NB. The body will be cremated and the Ashes taken to Australia.' In the winter of 1882, an England team, captained by the Hon. Ivo Bligh, toured Australia. England won a three-match series 2-1. According to legend, a group of Melbourne women burned a bail after that third Test, placed the ashes in a small urn, and presented them to Bligh as the `Ashes of England cricket'. The urn now stands on show in the Lord's museum and is competed for bi-annually. It was bequethed to MCC in the will of Lord Darnley (formerly Hon. Ivo Bligh) on his death in 1927. *See* **Lord's, MCC, Oval**.

asking rate

The rate at which a team is required to score runs in an innings to win a match.

assistance

Refers to a playing surface which favours the bowlers providing pace, bounce or spin.

Association of Cricket Umpires and Scorers (ACUS&S)

Governing body for cricket umpires and scorers. *See* **scorers and umpires**.

asterisk

Denotes a batman's not out score.

atmosphere

When heavy assists the ball to swing in the air. *See* swing.

'A' tour

Cricket tour embarked on by the shadow squad to the first team.

at stumps

The end of a day's play.

attack

A team's array of bowlers.

attack the batsman

Intimidatory field setting.

at the close (of play)

See at stumps.

at the crease

A batsman playing an innings.

at the wicket

See at the crease.

attitude

Mental approach to the game, usually reflected in the body language of a player.

Australia

One of the original countries of the International Cricket Council, then known as the Imperial Cricket Conference. It is now one of ten ICC full member countries comprising the international Test circuit. *See* **International Cricket Council, test circuit**.

Australian Cricket Board

The present board of control first met in May 1905. From 1909, the board was responsible for all Test tours to and from Australia. The Australian administration and its English counterpart were very different in approach. The Australian system involved almost every active cricketer on a democratic basis. Each cricket club which belonged to a colony (now state) cricket association elected representatives to the association and, in its turn, the association elected members to the Board of Control. In England, local cricketers and local cricket clubs had no say in the government of the game.

authentic stroke

A textbook shot. *See* **text book**.

averages

See **batting and bowling averages**.

away game

A match played away from the home ground.

away swing

A delivery that swings away in the air from a batsman. *See* **swing**.

B

back foot
The foot that is closer to the stumps when a batsman is at the crease. The right foot in the case of a right-handed batsman.

backing away
When the batsman takes a step to leg as the bowler delivers the ball.

backing up
Initial forward movement by non-striker at the point of delivery of the ball in anticipation of runs scored by the striking batsman. Also a fielder taking up a position to prevent overthrows. *See* **non-striker**.

backlift
The lift of the bat in a backwards direction by a batsman before releasing the bat forward into a shot.

back of a length
See short of a length.

back of the hand
A ball delivered by a wrist-spinner, with the back of his hand facing the ground at the point of release. *See* **wrist-spinner**.

back-to-back
Refers to successive victories or defeats or successive Test matches in a series with no matches between the end of the last Test and the beginning of the next.

backward defensive
A blocked shot played with the weight on the back foot and a straight bat.

backward of square
All fielding positions on the off and leg sides in an arc behind the striking batsman.

backward point
A close fielding position behind square on the off side. *See* **square**.

backward short leg
A close fielding position behind the batsman on the leg side.

backward square leg
A fielding position behind square on the leg side. *See* **square**.

bad ball
An inaccurate delivery from which runs may be scored without the likelihood of the batsman losing his wicket. *See* **loose delivery**.

badge
Team emblem providing a common identity.

bad light

The point at which the light has deteriorated so much that the umpires decree play must cease on grounds of safety. *See* **umpire**.

bag

Elongated, multi-pocketed sports grip used for carrying equipment. Also used in reference to wicket taking and catching - i.e. 'to bag three wickets.'

baggage-master

Individual responsible for the care of the player's equipment when on tour.

bagged a pair

A batsman making no runs in either innings of a match.

baggy green

Traditional style of cap worn by cricketers, synonymous with Australians.

bails

The two pieces of wood that balance on top of the three stumps at each end of the pitch.

Bakerloo Line

Colourful idiom referring to when a batsman plays down the wrong line.

balanced attack

A bowling line-up with variations of technique and style, allowing the captain options.

balanced side

Team with a bowling line-up which complements the batting potential.

ball

County and Test match balls are cased in red stitched leather, weighing not less than 5½oz/155.9g, nor more than 5¾oz/163g, and measuring not less than 8 13/16in/22.4cm, nor more than 9in/22.9cm in circumference. Duke & Son of Penshurst, Kent were the first manufacturers of cricket balls. Over the past 125 years there have been remarkably few modifications to the ball. A white ball is used in some limited-overs cricket.

ball doctoring

See ball tampering.

ball gauge

Device comprising two metal measuring rings for determining whether the ball has retained its shape.

balloon

A sharply rising ball either off the pitch or the bat.

ball sense

The ability to judge the length and pace of a ball quickly and deal with it effectively.

ball talk

A bowler's ability to conjure movement and life from a ball through the air or off the pitch to the detriment of the striking batsman.

ball tampering

Illegal change made to the shape or condition of the ball. It is illegal to rub the ball on the ground for any reason, interfere with any of the seams or the surface of the ball, use any implement, or take any other action which is likely to alter the condition of the ball. Allowed exceptions to this law include polishing the ball, removing mud and drying a wet ball on a towel.

balls to spare

A result achieved with time still remaining to finish the match.

bamboozled

Confused by the bowling.

banana ball

A swinging delivery.

Bangabandhu National Stadium

Bangladeshi Test match ground in Dhaka, the perimeter of which has a shopping centre and office accommodation.

bang in

Toughen the surface of a new bat with a special implement to prepare it for use. *See* **knocking in**.

Bangladesh

Given full membership of the ICC in 2000. After the partition of India, Bangladesh formed the eastern section of Pakistan until 1973, when Bangladesh became an independent nation. Several touring teams, including MCC, helped raise standards, and success in ICC Trophy tournaments led to their elevation to full ICC member status in 2000 and the prospect of a bright international future. *See* **International Cricket Council, MCC**.

baptism of fire

To make one's debut in a hostile or difficult environment.

Barabati Stadium

Occasionally-used Indian Test match ground close to the Mahal River in Cuttack.

Barmy Army

Unofficial, vocal body of predominantly young England supporters, seen regularly on winter tours overseas since The Ashes series in Australia in 1994–5. *See* **The Ashes**.

Basin Reserve

New Zealand Test match ground flanked by Mt Victoria to the east and Mt Cook to the west and located just a short walk from Wellington's central business district.

bat

Wooden implement for striking the ball. The official length of a bat shall be no more than 38in/96.5cm. The blade of the bat is made solely of willow and does not exceed 4¼in/10.8cm at its widest part. The first mention of the bat was made in a court case in 1613 when Nicholas Hockley assaulted Robert Hewett with a 'cricket staffe'.

bat cover

Protective travel / storage sheath, usually made from nylon.

bat coverings

Bindings preventing the grain of the willow from splitting and originally made from string and glue, but more likely to be fibreglass or gauze nowadays. *See* **willow**.

bat for lunch / tea

A batsman's conservative play in order to preserve his wicket until the interval.

bat-pad

Description of a delivery that first strikes the bat then the pad before it is taken by the catcher for a dismissal.

batsman's paradise

Playing surface which offers little assistance to the bowlers, allowing the batsman to score at will.

batsman's stance
The position of a batsman at the crease awaiting the delivery of a ball. *See* **crease**.

bat speed
The batsman's rapid hand action which generates the force of the shot.

bat through the innings (or carry his bat)
An opening batsman's success in managing to stay at the crease for an undefeated score right through an innings. *See* **at the crease**.

batting average
The average runs per innings of a batsman, achieved by dividing the number of runs scored by the number of completed innings played.

batting collapse
The rapid loss of wickets. Also known as the domino effect. *See* **crumble**.

batting order
The declared order in which the batsmen succeed one another after the loss of each wicket, varied occasionally by the state of play during the match.

batting wicket
Benign playing surface enabling the batsmen the opportunity to score plenty of runs.

beam ball
Australian for a full toss delivered at head height. *See* **beamer**.

beamer
An illegal high full-toss, delivered at speed and aimed at the batsman's head or upper body. *See* **full toss, beam ball**.

beaten for pace
When a pace bowler strikes the stumps or passes them with a delivery before a batsman has completed his stroke. *See* **pace bowler**.

beaten in the air
When a batsman is deceived by the flight of the ball. *See* **flight**.

beating the bat
A bowler's capacity to deliver a ball that passes the bat.

beat the field
A shot that dissects the fielding ring.

beer match
Friendly knockabout between two sides when the official match has been concluded well before the scheduled end of the day's play.

Bellerive Oval
Relatively young Australian Test ground located on the shores of the Derwent River in Tasmania. Playing conditions are often affected by Hobart's sea breezes.

belter
Excellent pitch conditions for batting on which a team is expected to make a big score.

benchmark
Level of achievement used as a point of reference in the comparison of individual and team performances.

benefit match
A game at which the spectators donate funds to a specific player or club.

benefit of the doubt
When an umpire decides to exercise his

BCCI: Board of Cricket Control for India

doubt about a decision in favour of the batsman.

benefit season
A testimonial year for a player. Generally granted to players capped by an English county for ten seasons or more. *See* **testimonial**.

benign pitch
A pitch surface offering little assistance to either batsman or bowler.

between bat and pad
Route of ball passing between a batsman's bat and pads.

Bhaji Army
English-based off-shoot of the Bharat Army.

Bharat Army
Indian version of the Barmy Army.

big match temperament
Refers to a player who has the ability to raise the level of his performance to equal the significance of the occasion.

bite
The amount of spin a bowler is able to induce from a pitch.

bit of bat on it
A batsman's success in managing to strike a near unplayable delivery with a small part of his bat.

Black Caps
Name by which the New Zealand national team is sometimes known and derived from their distinctive headgear which carries the white fern leaf motif.

blackwash
Play on the word 'whitewash', used to describe overwhelming Test series victory for West Indies. *See* **whitewash**.

blade
Alternative name for the bat.

Bligh, The Hon Ivo
See Ashes

blinder
Sometimes applied to a catch of extraordinary quality.

blindspot
Area where a batsman is unable to see the path of the ball, mainly due to the bowler going round the wicket.

blind swipe
Hit-and-hope swish by a batsman with eyes closed. Also known as a **yahoo**.

blob
A batsman's score of nought.

block
A defensive shot at which the ball is played forward with minimum force. Also the South African and Australian term for the square. *See* **square**.

blocker
A batsman more intent on guarding his stumps than endorsing adventurous stroke play.

blockhole
The small pit dug by batsmen in the popping crease when taking guard. *See* **guard, popping crease**

bodyline bowling

Sustained short-pitched bowling, supported by a large number of fielders in the short leg positions, and designed to strike the batsman's head or body. Also name given to England's tour of Australia in 1932–3 in which England's captain, Douglas Jardine, ordered his bowlers to adopt the tactic of bowling bouncers to try and hinder Bradman and the Australian batsmen from scoring runs. *See* **short of a length**.

bonus points

Awarded to teams in the English County Championship for batting and bowling achievements and adopted by Australia for its annual triangular one-day international tournament.

boots

Strong footwear worn by players, the sole often containing metal studs or spikes for better footing. Batting boots generally only have spikes on the ball of the foot.

Bosie

Australian term for leg-spin bowler's googly delivery. Named after the English cricketer B. T. Bosanquet, who invented it. *See* **googly, leg spin**.

Bothamesque

A feat of prodigious merit, worthy of former England all-rounder Ian Botham at his best with bat or ball.

bottom edge

A ball that strikes the lower edge of a bat when held in a horizontal position by a batsman during a shot.

bounce

The path of the ball after it has pitched.

bounce it in

Fielding method with the ball thrown to bounce before reaching the recipient in anticipation that it will be easier to take.

bouncer

A short-pitched ball delivered by a fast bowler at a batsman's head or upper body. *See* **short pitched**.

boundary

The edge of the playing area designated by a white line or rope. Also a shot producing four or six runs.

boundary rope

The marker used to denote the edge of the playing area. A white line is still used on some grounds.

Bourda Oval

West Indian Test match ground in Georgetown, Guyana. Its members' stand is more than 200 years old. A slow-paced wicket and a billiard table smooth outfield make it a batsman's paradise.

bowled

A ball that defeats a batsman and strikes his stumps.

bowler

See **seamer, spinner**.

bowler's benefit

Playing surface which provides pace, bounce, spin, seam and swing movement.

bowling analysis
See analysis.

bowling attack
See attack.

bowling average
See analysis.

bowling change
When one bowler is replaced by another.

bowling crease
Marked line next to the stumps.

bowling figures
See analysis.

bowling machine
Device used for batting practice that propels the ball at varying speeds and trajectories. Some are programmed to simulate spin.

bowling off the wrong foot
This is when the bowler takes off and lands on the same foot in the delivery stride.

bowling return
See analysis.

bowl seam up
A delivery released by the bowler with the seam in the vertical position.

box
Reinforced guard designed to protect the batsman's genitalia. Known as Hector Protector in Australia.

box office
A performance of outstanding entertainment value.

Bradman, Sir Donald
Recognised by Wisden in 2000 as the best player ever when voted top of a poll for the 'Five Cricketers of the Century'. Played 52 Tests for Australia, scoring 6,996 runs at an average of 99.94. He was knighted in 1949 for his services to the game. *See* **Wisden**.

bread and butter shot
An easy scoring delivery often referred to as meat and drink.

breadbasket
A catch that goes straight to hand.

breeze
An easy victory, or a wind that may assist certain bowlers.

bridesmaid
A mild slight attributed to the beaten side.

Brisbane Oval
Australian Test match ground built on swamp land and known as 'The 'Gabba' was established in 1895 when it was leased to the Queensland Cricket Association. *See* **Queensland Cricket Association**.

Broadhalfpenny Down
Historic cricket ground at Hambledon, Hampshire, known as 'the cradle of cricket.' The Broadhalfpenny Brigands Cricket Club have been running cricket on Broadhalfpenny Down for more than forty years. The ground is owned by the Brigands and Winchester College and stands opposite the famous 'Bat and Ball' Inn, which contains a fine collection of cricket memorabilia.

broken wicket

The stumps and bails are disturbed for an attempted run out. *See* **run out**.

Brumbrella

Motorised unfolding ground cover first used by Warwickshire CCC at Edgbaston. *See* **Edgbaston, Warwickshire CCC**.

buffet ball

A ball so poorly delivered it encourages the batsman to help himself. *See* **cafeteria bowling**.

bullet

Used in relation to a delivery of extreme pace.

bump ball

Shot hit directly into the ground, sometimes giving the impression of offering a catch if it carries to a fielder.

bumper

See **bouncer**.

bungled

Refers to a failed run out attempt.

bunny

Used to describe a batsman who is regularly dismissed by the same bowler.

Bunsen burner

Rhyming slang (turner) used to describe a pitch that is taking spin.

burn out

Physical or mental fatigue induced by excessive and sustained exertion.

Busta Cup

West Indian version of the County Championship.

butter-fingers

Player inept at catching the ball.

bye

A delivery that passes the bat, without contact made, and the wicket-keeper, allowing a run(s) to be scored. *See* **extras**.

C

cabbage patch
An inferior playing surface on which to bat. Also known as a cart track and a minefield.

cack-hander
See left-hander.

cafeteria bowling
Poor bowling of the help yourself variety. Also known as canteen cricket.

call
Verbal exchange between batsmen when deciding whether to attempt a run; an umpire's shout of 'no ball' to denote an illegal delivery; the toss-up at the start of the match at which the home captain spins the coin and invites his opposite number to call 'heads' or 'tails.' *See* **no ball, toss up.**

call up
The selection of a player for a team or squad.

calypso cricket
Unorthodox style of play associated with the West Indians and symbolised by aggressive, cavalier play.

camping in
Said of a batsman determined to protect his wicket, but not prepared to attack the bowling.

Canada
Entered the ICC Trophy in 1979 and a

participant in that tournament ever since. Toronto staged a series of one-day internationals between India and Pakistan in 1996. More than 10,000 adults play cricket in the country. *See* **ICC Trophy.**

can't buy a run
Derogatory remark reflecting a batsman's poor form.

canteen cricket
See **cafeteria bowling, buffet ball.**

cap
An award given to a player for successfully completing his apprenticeship. English county players are 'capped' when achieving first-class standards after a period of service. A Test player is awarded his cap on debut.

caps
Traditional headgear worn by players. Advent of the floppy-hat and helmets have supplemented headwear.

captain
The player in charge of the team.

captain's innings, a
An innings of outstanding merit played by a captain when his team is in trouble.

captain's role
Combination of responsibilities including

leading the team's effort on the pitch, deciding and implementing tactics and performing an ambassadorial function.

Carisbrook

New Zealand Test match ground in Dunedin which sits in the entrance to a steep-sided valley and is flanked on two sides by the main South Island railway. The most southerly Test ground in the world.

Carmody field

Named after Keith Carmody, the New South Wales and Western Australia player who originated the 'umbrella' field, a semi-circle of close catchers set between wicket-keeper and point. *See* umbrella.

carried his bat

See **bat through the innings**.

carry

The trajectory a ball takes when it has passed a batsman. Can also be defined as whether a ball passes to the fielder from the batsman all the way in the air. If it bounces first then it did not carry.

cart track

See **cabbage patch**.

castle(d)

Australian for the stumps. To be bowled.

catch

Ball held by fielder to dismiss batsman after it has struck bat or glove and travelled into his hands without touching the ground.

catches win matches

Old and wise saying to point out that a team holding its catches will triumph more than a side that spills chances.

caught and bowled

Catch held by bowler off his own bowling to dismiss batsman.

caught behind

Catch held by wicket-keeper to dismiss batsman.

caution

Prudent care. Also umpire's warning to the bowler for excessive hostile deliveries and bowler or batsman for running on the wicket.

celebrity side

A team of well-known people from all walks of life.

central contracts

Contractual agreement between a cricket board and an international player of that country. England adopted the system recently to pay their Test and one-day international players from a central fund and have more control over their playing commitments.

century

A hundred or more runs. *See* **hundred, ton**.

cessation of play

End of play.

chabuk batting

Indian for an aggressive but controlled batting performance.

chain

Archaic unit of linear measure of 22 yards, the length of a cricket pitch.

championship

The main domestic First-Class county competition, comprising two innings. *See* **First Class match**.

championship match

A First-Class county match. *See* **First Class**.

chance

A catching opportunity. Also the squandered opportunity of a stumping or run out.

change bowler

Player used for a single over to enable the current bowlers to alternate ends.

channel

See **corridor of uncertainty**.

charge

A batsman demonstrating aggressive instincts against a bowler to increase the run-rate, as in 'give it the charge'. *See* **run rate**.

chassé

A batsman's shuffle across the crease.

cheap runs

Allowing batsmen to score easily, primarily through poor bowling or fielding. *See* **leading runs.**

cheat

To play outside the Laws of the game.

check

When a ball slows down unexpectedly off the pitch, often causing the batsman to mistime his shot.

check drive

A punched shot with a straight-faced bat.

Cheltenham & Gloucester Trophy

One-day competition with a Lord's final, formerly known as the Nat-West Trophy, the origins of which were in the Gillette Cup.

cherry

Euphemism for cricket ball. Also the mark left on the bat by the ball.

chest pad

Protection for the rib region.

Chinaman

The left-arm wrist spinner's googly. *See* **googly, wrist spinner**.

Chinese cut

A shot that flies off the inside edge of the bat to long leg. Also known as a French cut, and Harrow drive. *See* **long leg**.

chin music

Colloquialism for intimidatory bowling that threatens a batsman's head.

chip shot

A crafted aerial stroke played without force.

chirping

Verbal attempts by the fielders to unsettle the batsmen. *See* **sledging.**

Chittagong

Bangladeshi Test match ground, used by East Pakistan before Bangladesh became an independent nation.

chucker

A bowler outlawed for throwing. *See* **throwing**.

chucking

chucking
A bowler who throws illegally. Can also refer to losing a match.

circle
Inner cordon of fielders.

clap in
The traditional welcome of the incoming batsmen by the fielding team.

class act
A performance of exceptional quality.

clean bowled
A ball that strikes the wicket without hitting the bat, pads or any part of the batsman's body.

clip
Batting shot, usually played off the toes from a half volley in the direction of square leg. *See* **half volley, square leg**.

close of play
The end of the day's play.

close out a game
A team's ability to capitalise on a winning position.

closing the face
Angling the main hitting surface of the bat towards the batsman's pads.

club cricket
Matches played at a variety of levels beneath the professional game.

clutch situation
Period of play pivotal to the outcome of a match.

coaching
Tuition in batting, bowling, fielding, wicket-keeping and other aspects of the game of cricket.

coat of varnish
Used to describe a bowler's near miss of the wickets by the narrowest of margins.

coconut matting
Artificial playing surface made out of the fibre from coconut husks.

code of conduct
Document signed by every professional player declaring an obligation to report any suspicious behaviour or corrupt approach.

coffin
A large, solid-sided bag for carrying kit. *See* **kit**.

collapse
See **batting collapse**.

colts
Junior members of a cricket club.

coming on
Term used to describe a delivery that hurries off the pitch onto the batsman.

coming through
Bowler's request to bowl round the wicket between the stumps and the umpire.

competitions
The programme of matches for a season.

compo
Australian for a ball made from a composite of cork and rubber.

composure
Relaxed state of mind of a player in command of his emotions.

concentration
Prerequisite in all aspects of the game, but particularly relevant to a batsman trying to fathom the bowler's intentions and protect his wicket.

Condon, Lord Paul
Former Metropolitan Police Commissioner and head of the International Cricket Council's anti-corruption squad, founded in 2000. *See* International Cricket Council.

Conduit Fields
By which the playing area of Lord's cricket ground is sometimes known. *See* Lord's.

confidence
A belief in one's own ability which can evaporate without warning.

controlled aggression
Used to describe a player who channels his aggressive instincts and energy into his performance.

cordon
A circle of fielders surrounding the batsman on strike.

corker
An outstanding delivery. Also a practice ball made from cork.

corridor of uncertainty
A narrow channel on or about the batsman's off-stump, that is said to cause doubt in the striking batsman's mind.

County Championship
The main domestic first-class competition in England now played over four days per match.

county cricket
The name for the professional game played by the eighteen English counties.

county match
A first-class match, of four days duration, played in the English County Championship. *See* County Championship.

cover(s)
The area of the field on the off-side between point and mid-off. *See* mid-off, point.

cover drive
A stroke played off the front or back foot that propels the ball through the area between point and mid-off. *See* mid-off, point.

covering the pitch
Laying protective equipment on the pitch when play is not in progress to protect it from rain. Before the 1960s, pitches were generally uncovered during a match. *See* sticky dog.

covering the stumps
Batsman's use of bat or pads to screen the stumps from a bowler's delivery.

cover point
Fielding position on the off side between mid-off and gully. *See* mid-off, gully.

covers
Mobile equipment designed to protect the pitch or square from the elements when play is not in progress.

cow corner
An area of the boundary between mid-wicket and long on that is favoured by batsmen of limited ability who prefer to strike across the line rather than hit straight. *See* **across the line**.

cow shot
See **cow corner**.

cracks in the pitch
Fissures in the playing surface that can be exploited by the bowlers to the detriment of the batting side.

cradle
Device used to practice slip catches.

cradle of cricket, the
Widely regarded as the Broadhalfpenny Down ground, Hambledon, on which the Broadhalfpenny Brigands play their matches.

cramped for room
Limited space for a batsman in which to give free rein to a shot.

crazy paving
Description given to the appearance of a cracked playing surface. *See* **cracks in the pitch.**

crease
The batting crease and popping crease.

Cricinfo
Commercial organisation providing cricket information on the world wide web and a former sponsor of the County Championship. *See* **County Championship**.

cricket
Contest between two teams of 11-a-side playing on a pitch 22 yards long. The game derives its curious name from an old French word, *criquet*, describing the sound made by a ball striking wood.

cricket colours
Badge or tie awarded by schools to pupils who have excelled at cricket.

Cricketer International, The
Monthly cricket magazine founded in 1921 by Sir Pelham 'Plum' Warner.

Cricket Foundation, The
Charitable organisation founded in 1982 and devoted to the development of the game.

cricket nations
Countries who play cricket .

Cricket World Cup
Tournament of one-day matches between countries. First held in England in 1975 and played there every four years until 1987, when it was hosted jointly by India and Pakistan. Now shared around the world in a four-year cycle.

crocked
Australian slang for a player unable to participate due to injury.

cross bat
A shot played across the line of the ball. *See* **across the line**.

crowd
Intimidatory deployment of fielders around the bat.

crumble

Deterioration of a pitch, usually through sustained use and common towards the end of a match. Also a batting collapse.

curator

See groundsman.

curtain rail shot

Inelegant swishing batting stroke played across the front of the lower legs.

custard arm

Colourful Australian description of a fielder with a weak throwing arm.

cut shot

A shot played to a short ball with a horizontal bat in which the ball is normally dispatched square or behind square on the off side. *See* square.

cutter

A delivery bowled at pace which moves into the batsman off the pitch or jags away from the batsman towards the off side.

crumble

D

dab

Defensive half-shot in which the ball is pushed a short distance to the off or leg side.

daisy cutter

A ball that fails to bounce normally and skims low across the surface.

damaged ball

A ball with a broken or damaged seam or segment of surface.

damaging the pitch

Surface of pitch illegally scuffed up by bowler or fielders.

dance down the wicket

See down the wicket.

danger area

A ball pitched into a zone which presents most difficulty for the batsman.

dangerous and unfair bowling

Intimidatory bowling that contravenes Law 42 governing fair and unfair play.

day night game

A one-day match that begins in daylight and ends under floodlights. *See* one-day match.

dead ball

The ball is considered 'dead' when it is clear to the umpire at the bowler's end that the fielding side and both batsmen have ceased to regard it as in play. *See* umpire.

dead bat

A defensive shot played with no power that drops the ball in the crease.

dead wicket

A pitch which offers little bounce or lateral movement.

death rattle

The sound of the ball striking the wickets signalling the end of a batsman's innings.

declaration bowler

A bowler of limited ability deployed to concede as many runs as possible in the shortest time to encourage a declaration. *See* declared.

declared / declaration

Decision by the captain of the batting side to close an innings at any time during a match.

deep

Fielding areas close to the boundaries.

deep extra cover

Fielding position to the right of cover and the left of mid-off, positioned deep to cut off shots to the cover boundary.

deep fine leg

See fine leg.

deep mid-wicket
Fielding position between square leg and mid-on, positioned deep to cut off shots to the leg-side boundary. *See* **boundary**.

deep point
Fielding position square with the wicket on the off side, positioned deepish between gully and cover point. *See* **gully**.

deep square leg
Fielding position square with the wicket on the leg side, positioned between long leg and mid-wicket ostensibly to cut off pull shots to the boundary. *See* **boundary, pull shot**.

deliberate distraction
Wilful attempt by any member of the fielding side to distract or obstruct either batsman after the striker has received the ball.

delivery
A ball bowled at the striking batsman.

delivery stride
The step or leap that the bowler takes as he bowls the ball.

Derbyshire CCC
The present club was established on 4 November, 1870. The county was admitted to the official County Championship in 1895. The club colours are chocolate, amber and pale blue. The badge is a rose and crown. Ground: Race Course Ground, Derby.

devil's number
An Australian superstition involving the number 87, 13 short of a hundred.

diamond duck
A dismissal first ball of the match.

dibbly dobbly bowlers
Tactical use of unrecognised bowlers, usually to stem the flow of runs or break a batting partnership.

did not bat
Batsman not required to bat when an innings has ended prematurely.

die(d)
Used in relation to a ball which fails to bounce after pitching.

dig, first / second
Alternative term for innings.

dig in
Defiant innings with the batsman's focus on survival rather than run scoring.

dil se
The Indian expression for a bowler with rhythm and accuracy.

disciplinary committee
Body established to maintain good standards of behaviour.

disciplines
Individual areas of skill used in the collective sense.

dismissal
The removal of a batsman.

dissent
Refusal to accept umpire's verdict or decision made by other appointed match officials. *See* **umpire**.

dobber
A bowler of no great pace, but accurate.

doing the tins
To work the scoreboard. Originated during the time when painted tin plates were used to register the score.

dolly
A simple catch.

domino effect
Rapid collapse of an innings.

done up like a kipper
A batsman comprehensively deceived by a delivery.

donkey drop
A high, lobbed delivery by a bowler.

Dorothy Dicks
Rhyming slang for a six.

dot ball
A ball that prevents a batsman from scoring.

Double Wicket World Cup
Limited-over competition with two-man teams representing eight Test playing countries.

down the ground
A ground or aerial shot played towards the boundary that travels between mid-off and mid-on.

down the wicket
A batsman's advance down the pitch to attack or defend.

drags on to stumps
A ball deflected onto the stumps by a batsman attempting a shot.

draw
A match in which a victory is not achieved by either side.

drawn stumps
End of the day's play.

dream team
An imaginary group of players chosen for their specific individual skills.

dressing room
Off-limit area in the pavilion restricted to the use of players.

drift
Delivery that floats in the opposite direction to the spin imparted by the bowler.

drinks break
Interval for refreshments taken on the field of play.

drive
A shot played with the full swing of a perpendicular bat to dispatch the ball through the off or on sides, either square or in front of the wicket. *See* **square**.

drop in pitch (wicket)
Substitute playing surface prepared and cultivated off site, usually employed when the ground is used for other sporting activies.

dropped
Discarded from the team; a missed catch.

dry over
An over in which no runs are conceded. *See* **maiden**.

Domestic Structure Review Group (DSRG)

duck

A score of no runs.

Duckworth/Lewis method

Sets revised targets in rain-interrupted limited-overs matches in accordance with the relative run scoring resources which are at the disposal of the two sides.

Duke & Son

The first manufacturers of cricket balls. *See* ball.

Duke of Norfolk's XI

Team invited to play at Arundel against the Australians in the traditional curtain-raiser to an Ashes series.

dug in

An obdurate batting partnership remarkable more for its longevity than run aggregate.

Durham CCC

Formation of the present club was 10 May, 1882. The county was officially admitted to the County Championship in 1992. The club colours are navy blue, yellow and maroon. The badge is the coat of arms of the county of Durham. Ground: Riverside, Chester-le-Street. *See* Riverside.

duck

DOOSRA
Derived from the Hindi for 'the other way', a ball from an off-spinner projected out of the back of the hand which skids straight on or spins the other way.

E

easy paced
A benign playing surface.

easy single
A run taken at the pace of an amble with little risk of a run out.

economy rate
Average number of runs conceded by a bowler per over.

Eden Gardens
India's premier Test match ground in Calcutta and noted for attracting crowds in excess of 100,000.

Eden Park
Unusually shaped New Zealand Test match ground in Auckland with peculiar angled boundaries. Primarily a rugby stadium, it has used drop-in pitches to stage cricket matches.

Edgbaston
English Test match ground in Birmingham and headquarters of Warwickshire County Cricket Club. The first ground in the country to implement the use of floodlights for day/night one-day matches. *See* **day/night, one-day match, Warwickshire CCC.**

edge
The edge of the blade of the bat.

effort ball
The sudden injection of extra pace into a delivery by a bowler to the surprise of the batsman.

egg and bacon tie
Colloquial description of the official tie worn by members of the Marylebone Cricket Club, the two primary colours being red and yellow. *See* **MCC.**

eleven
See XI.

élite panel
Group of eight Test match umprires nominated by the International Cricket Council.

end holder
A bowler whose primary function is to bowl accurately and economically, thereby exacting pressure on the batsmen while a bowler with more wicket taking potential operates from the other end.

ends
The two opposite points on the wicket where the stumps are located.

England
With Australia, the originators of Test cricket. Tests began in 1876–7 when two matches were played in Australia, the home side winning the first, England the second.

English Premier League (EPL)

England and Wales Cricket Board (ECB)

Became responsible for the administration of all cricket – professional and recreational – in England and Wales on 1 January, 1997. It took over the functions of the Cricket Council, the old Test and County Cricket Board and the National Cricket Association, which had run the game since 1968. The Management Board is answerable to the First-Class Forum on matters concerning the first-class game and to the Recreational Forum on affairs relating to the non-professional game.

English Schools Cricket Association

Governing body of schools' cricket.

Essex CCC

Formation of the present club was 14 January 1876. The county was officially admitted to the County Championship in 1895. The club colours are blue, gold and red. The badge is three seaxes above a scroll bearing the county name. Ground: County Ground, Chelmsford.

ethics committee

A first-class team's self regulatory body monitoring dissent, violence and corruption.

European Cricket Council (ECC)

Superseded the old European Cricket Federation in June 1997. In 2000, the Council consisted of England (Full Member); Denmark, France, Germany, Gibraltar, Ireland, Israel, Italy, Netherlands and Scotland (Associate Members); and Austria, Belgium, Cyprus, Czech Republic, Finland, Greece, Luxembourg, Malta, Norway, Portugal, Spain, Sweden and Switzerland (Affiliate Members).

expensive over

An over in which a bowler has been hit for a large number of runs.

extra cover

Fielding position on the off side between cover point and mid-off. *See* **cover point**.

extra fine

A fielding position behind square on the off or leg side that is more acute than an angle of 45 degrees with the pitch. *See* **square**.

extra half hour

Time allowed at the end of a day's play to enable the match to be completed when the result appears inevitable.

extras

Runs added to a side's innings that are not scored off the bat, e.g. byes, leg byes, wides and no-balls; known as sundries in Australia.

F

face
The surface of the bat used for striking the ball.

facing
Refers to the batsman on strike awaiting the next bowling delivery.

failure
Unrespectable score by a front line batsman.

faint edge
A delivery that has struck a wafer-thin edge of the bat.

fair delivery
Relates to the bowler's stride which requires the front foot to land behind the popping crease and the back foot within, but not touching, the return crease. *See* **popping crease, return crease**.

fair play
This notion is synonymous with the game of cricket and resulted in the introduction in to the English language of the phrases 'It's not cricket', 'Play the game', etc. whenever the laws or the spirit of the game have been transgressed.

fall of wicket
The runs scored in a side's innings at the moment one of the ten wickets falls.

false stroke
A poor shot induced by a testing delivery.

farming the strike
A batsman's deliberate attempt to hog the bowling and protect a weaker batsman from facing the bowler(s).

fast bowlers' union
See **quick bowlers' club**.

feather
The faintest of touches by the bat on the ball.

featherbed
A benign pitch surface offering a bowler the minimum bounce, pace or movement.

feeling for the ball
A shot played by a batsman at a wide delivery when not in full control of the stroke. *See* **fishing, flashing**.

feet in concrete shot
Indecisive and often a poorly played stroke caused by the batsman failing to move his feet into the correct position.

Feroz Shah Kotla
Compact Indian Test match venue at Delhi and regarded as batsman-friendly due to the docile nature of its pitches.

ferret
Fielder known for his electrifying movement, i.e. pick-up and throw. Also poor batsman who comes to the wicket last after the rabbits (only slightly more talented batsmen) have been dismissed. *See* **rabbits.**

fetch a delivery
When a batsman has to reach for the ball.

fielding
The art of stopping, retrieving, catching and throwing a ball when struck by the batsman.

fielding arc
The deployment of players in a circle to cut off boundary strokes or shots for singles. *See* **single**.

fielding positions
Points close to the stumps or in the outfield where the fielders are positioned. *See* **outfield**.

fielding the ball
Stopping or catching the ball.

field of play
The playing arena inside the boundary edge.

fiery
Pace bowler with intimidatory instincts.

fifty
The first run-making milestone that a batsman strives to reach.

fighting spirit
A team or individual's resolve not to capitulate in the face of adversity.

figures
Bowler's analysis. *See* **analysis**

Fiji
The game was first played there in 1874. Founding father of cricket was the Attorney-General J.S. Udal. Elected an associate member of ICC in 1965. Regular participants in the ICC Trophy competitions. *See* **ICC Trophy**.

fill your boots
Batsman's opportunity to take advantage of favourable conditions to score a plentiful supply of runs.

fine edge
A thin, nicked edge.

fine leg
Fielding position behind the striking batsman between the wicket-keeper and square leg. Short fine leg is used to prevent the batsman running a single. Deep fine leg allows the batsman to take a single but prevents a boundary. *See* **boundary, deep, single**.

finger spinner
A bowler who uses his fingers primarily to impart spin on the ball.

first change
The third bowler used in an innings to replace one of the two opening bowlers. *See* **opening bowler**.

First-Class match
Describes the status of a match. Applied to Tests, county championship, provincial, state, and some other fixtures, but excluding matches of limited-over duration.

first eleven

The senior team in a club that fields more than one side.

first slip

Fielding position next to the wicket-keeper on the off side.

fishing

An ill-conceived shot in which a batsman plays away from his body, reaching for the ball with his bat when not in control of the stroke. *See* **feeling for the ball**.

five out, all out

Adage suggesting that an innings is all but over once the first five wickets have fallen.

flannels

Cricket trousers. Also known as whites.

flap

An unsuccessful and technically poor catching attempt.

flashing

An attacking, air shot where the batsman has failed to make contact.
See **air shot**.

flatbat

Unorthodox stroke played with a horizontal bat.

flat track

Pitch offering conditions conducive to run-making.

flat track bully

Term applied to batsman better suited to scoring runs when conditions are ideal than achieving success when the bowling or conditions are difficult.

flicked away

Wristy shot for runs played with minimum of bat movement.

flicx pitch

Mobile plastic wicket developed for use in South African townships.

flier

Rapid run-making start to an innings. *See* **pinch hitter**.

flight

Lofted bowling delivery used in an attempt to get movement or drift in the air and surprise the striking batsman.

flighted ball

Slow delivery of high trajectory tossed up at a batsman.

flighted delivery

See **flighted ball**.

flincher

A batsman uncomfortable at facing quick bowling.

flip

An underarm shy at the stumps.

flipper

Part of leg spinner's armoury, a delivery squeezed out of the front of the hand between thumb and fingers, of flat trajectory that skids off the pitch. Originated by the Australian Bowler C. V. Grimmett in the 1930s. *See* **leg spinner**.

floater
See arm ball.

floppy hat
See caps.

flying slip
Occasionally used fielding position in line with a conventional slip but closer to the boundary in the likelihood of securing a top edge catch.

focused
A state of mind above the level of concentration.

follow on
In a two-innings match of five days or more, the side which bats first and leads by at least 200 runs shall have the option of requiring the other side to follow their innings. The same option shall be available in two-innings matches of shorter duration with the minimum required leads as follows: (a) 150 runs in a match of three or four days; (b) 100 runs in a two-day match; (c) 75 runs in a one-day match.

follow through
The culmination of a bowler's forward momentum after delivery of the ball.

foothold
The point at which a bowler's front foot stamps down during delivery. Sawdust helps achieve better adhesion on a rain affected surface.

foot hole
Area around the crease which has been churned up by the bowler's spikes.

footwear
See boots

footwork
Use of feet by a batsman when playing a stroke.

form
A player's current level of performance.

Forty Club, The
Wandering club founded in 1936 with the object of bringing amateur and professional players together when county days were done. Its members are spread all over the world with a long programme of matches played every year and an annual dinner that draws upwards of 1,000 members. Presidents have included Sir Pelham Warner, Sir Jack Hobbs, Gubby Allen and Herbert Sutcliffe. The club's patron is the Duke of Edinburgh.

forward defensive
A block played with the weight on the front foot and a straight bat.

forward lunge
Ill-disciplined, uncontrolled stroke played off balance off the front foot.

forward push
Fencing at the ball off the front foot with minimum backlift.

found the boundary
A shot that crosses the boundary rope for four runs.

found the edge
A bowler's success in striking the edge of the bat with a delivery.

floater

found the fielder
A good batting shot from which runs are unable to be taken as it was played straight to a fielder.

found the gap
A shot that punctures the field.

four
A shot to the boundary for four runs.

fourth umpire
Usually the substitute umpire.

free hit
A free shot granted to a batsman in which he cannot be bowled or caught.

Freemantle Doctor
A sea breeze which assists bowlers at the Western Australia Cricket Ground in Perth. *See* **Western Australia Cricket Ground**.

French cut
See **Chinese cut**.

fringe bowler
Occasional bowler whose primary function in the team is more likely to be as a batsman.

Frizzel
Financial services company and sponsors of the English County Championship.

front foot no ball
An unfair delivery occurs when the bowler's front foot, whether grounded or raised, passes beyond the popping crease. *See* **popping crease**.

front foot player
A batsman favouring forward play rather than making shots off the back foot.

front line bowlers
Those with the greatest wicket taking potential.

full bunger
Australian equivalent of a full toss.

full house
A bowler's haul of five wickets or more in an innings. *See* **Michelle**. Also a capacity crowd.

full length
A ball delivered up to the batsman.

full toss
A legitimate delivery that reaches the batsman without bouncing.

future tours programme (FTP)

G

Gabba, The
See Brisbane Oval.

Gaddafi Stadium
Well appointed Pakistan Test match ground in
the city of Lahore, following a major renovation
for the 1996 World Cup.

Galle National Stadium
Sri Lankan ground close to the sea in the city
of Galle, south of Colombo, and given Test
status in 1998.

game plan
Pre-conceived method designed to defeat an
opposing player or team, often achieved
through the exploitation of a particular
weakness.

gamesmanship
Intimidation of an opponent in an attempt to
gain advantage. This offence is governed by
Law 42, which deals with 'fair and Unfair
Play.'

gardening
Removing divots and flattening the pitch with
bat or hand to improve the surface.

gate, the
The paid attendance at a match.

gate, through the
A delivery that passes between bat and pad.

gazunder
Australian slang for a ball which goes under
the bat.

get a bag
Derogatory Australian remark directed at a
player who has dropped a catch.

get a big stride in
Phrase used to describe a positive step down
the wicket to meet the ball and reduce the risk
of a leg before wicket dismissal.

gismo
American slang for gadgetry applied to cricket
aids such as radar equipment for monitoring
the speed of a bowler's delivery.

given out
A batsman's dismissal signalled by the umpire.

giving it the charge
Used to describe an aggressive batsman who
advances down the pitch as or after the
bowler has released the ball.

giving the ball air
See air.

Glamorgan CCC

Formation of the present club 6 July 1888. Admitted to the County Championship in 1921. The colours are blue and gold. The badge is a gold daffodil. Ground: Sophia Gardens, Cardiff.

glance

A stroke diverted fine behind square. *See* square.

Gloucestershire CCC

Formation of the present club was in 1871. The club was an original member of the County Championship with the legendary W.G. Grace in its ranks. The club colours are blue, gold, brown, silver, green and red. The badge is the coat of arms of the city and county of Bristol. Ground: County Ground, Bristol.

gloved–it

A delivery diverted from the stump area by a batsman's glove rather than bat.

gloveman

Colloquialism for wicket keeper.

gloves

Padded protective mittens worn by batsmen and wicket-keepers.

goes to hand

A ball that carries to a fielder without bouncing.

gogga

(pronounced googa) South Africa term used to describe an unorthodox bowling action and derived from the ungainly gait of the gogga bug.

golden duck

Batsman's dismissal first ball for nought.

golden pair

Batsman's dismissal first ball in each innings.

goli

Indian for good fielding.

gone for all money

Australian phrase used to describe a batting failure.

goober

Australian for a simple catch.

good arm

Description of a player with the ability to throw the ball powerfully and accurately.

good hands

Term applied to fielder or wicket-keeper adept at making catches.

good length ball

A delivery that, on pitching, raises doubt in the batsman's mind as to whether to play forward or back.

Goodyear Park

The most recently approved of South Africa's Test match grounds in Bloemfontein.

googly

An off-break bowled with a leg-break action. A left-hand bowler's googly turns from leg to off Also known as wrong 'un or Bosie. *See* leg break, off break.

got a lot of wood on it
Used to describe a batsman hitting the ball with tremendous force.

got big
A delivery that arrives at the batsman with more pace and bounce than anticipated.

got his eye in
Batsman's acclimatisation to the bowling.

got off the mark
Said of a batsman after scoring his opening run/s.

governing bodies
Ruling cricket boards of respective countries.

Grace, W.G.
The most famous cricketer of all time. Born in Gloucestershire in 1848, he captained the county of his birth for 25 years. A legendary batsman, he scored the 126th and last century of his career on his 56th birthday. Played 22 Tests for England. He died in 1915.

grade cricket
Club cricket in Australia. *See* club cricket.

grass roots cricket
Informal structure promoting the growth of the game.

green
Pitch colouring suggesting a moist surface giving assistance to seam bowlers.

green light
Illuminated signal used by the third umpire from the pavilion conveying that a batsman is not out. *See* pavilion, umpire.

Green Park
Picturesque but, due to India's rotation system, little used Test match ground in the heart of Kanpur.

green surface
A well grassed pitch of help to seam bowlers. Also known as a greentop. *See* seam bowler.

greentop
See green surface.

grill
Facial protection on a helmet.

grip
Manner in which the batsman holds the bat; also the rubber cover for the bat handle.

groin injury
Pain in pelvic area caused by injury.

groove, in the
The achievement of consistency, primarily of a bowler, but also a batsman after a period of settling in.

ground
Generic term used to describe the venue, including the playing area.

grounded
To ground the toe of the bat. Also used in reference to a dropped catch.

ground fielding
Run, pick up and throw from the square or outfield.

groundsman
Official responsible for pitch, outfield and

ground maintenance. Known as a curator in Australia.

ground the bat

Batsman's quick reaction to anchor his bat to the ground to avoid stumping or run out. *See* **run out, stumping**.

grubber

A delivery that runs along the ground after pitching.

guard

The bat position for a batsman's stance. 'Centre' denotes a batsman's request to an umpire for a middle stump guard; 'two legs' denotes the request for a middle-and-leg guard; 'off-stump' denotes guard to cover the off stump.

gully

Fielding position behind square between point and slip. *See* **point, slip, square**.

half-cock shot
A stroke played with a half forward movement.

half-pitcher
Australian equivalent of the short ball.

half rubbers
Type of batting boot with spikes only on the ball of the foot.

half tracker
Short pitched delivery. *See* **short pitched**.

half volley
Delivery over-pitched enticing batsman to attack. *See* **over-pitched**.

Hambledon
Village in Hampshire acknowledged as the 'cradle of cricket.' The club was formed in the mid-1700s with matches played on Broadhalfpenny Down, opposite the famous 'Bat and Ball' Inn.

Hampshire CCC
The club was established on 12 August 1863. Admitted to the County Championship in 1895. The club colours are blue, gold and white. The badge is a Tudor rose and crown. Ground: Since 2001, Rose Bowl, West End, Southampton.

hamstring injury
Tendon injury at the back of the knee

hand action
Bowler's manipulation of the ball at the point of delivery to create movement and energy on the ball. *See* **movement**.

handled the ball
Law 33 dismissal for batsman found guilty of wilfully touching the ball with hand(s) without consent of opposing side.

hand signals
The umpire's signals to denote out, six runs, four runs, bye, leg-bye, wide, no ball, dead ball, one short (run), etc. *See* **umpire**.

hanging the bat out to dry
A shot played wide of the body with no conviction, no control, and no footwork. *See* **footwork**.

Harare Sports Club
Test match ground regarded as the home of cricket in Zimbabwe.

hard ball
Used to describe a ball that hits the bat with a jarring velocity.

hard bat
Resilience factor determined by the width of the grain of the willow used in the manufacture of bats, a wide grain generally producing a hard bat and a narrow grain a soft bat.

Harrow bat
Bat one size down from adult bat, used by schoolboy players.

Harrow drive
Poorly executed off drive, resulting in the ball's unintentional deflection off the inside edge of the bat. *See* **off drive**.

hat-trick
Three wickets in three successive balls by ythe same bowler. Originated in the formative years of the game when, after taking three wickets in three consecutive deliveries, a bowler would be awarded a new top hat, *de rigueur* for cricketers in those days.

haul
Relates to the number of wickets taken in a match by a single bowler.

have a blow
Captain's instruction to end a bowler's current spell. *See* **spell**.

have a go
To attack the bowling.

Hawk-eye
Electronic gadgetry used by television cricket broadcasters to adjudge leg before wicket decisions. *See* **Skyscope**.

Headingley
English Test match ground in Leeds and headquarters of Yorkshire County Cricket Club. *See* **Yorkshire CCC**.

heavy bails
Are weighted with lead to prevent them from being dislodged in windy playing conditions.

heavy ball
A delivery propelled at exceptional pace.

heavy roller
Groundsman's equipment for flattening pitch surface. *See* **groundsman**.

Hector Protector
Australian for the box. *See* **box.**

held up
A ball that goes straight on when it is expected to move sideways.

helmet
Protective headguard worn by batsmen and fielders close to the wicket.

help yourself variety
See **buffet ball**.

Heyhoe-Flint, Rachael
See **women's cricket**.

high action
A bowling technique with the delivery arm as near vertical as possible and a trait of off spinners, seamers and swing bowlers.

high and handsome
A batsman's lofted shot over the fielding cordon.

hit against the spin
Striking the ball in the opposite direction to which it is turning.

hit out
Instruction to batsman to increase run-getting

tempo at the risk of losing his wicket in the process.

hitter
Aggressive run-scorer with ability to raise run-rate. *See* **run-rate, pinch hitter**.

hit the ball twice
Law 34 governing form of dismissal for batsman striking ball twice with his bat or person.

hit the pad
Ball striking batsman's pad.

hitting across the line
A cross-batted shot across the line of the approaching delivery. *See* **across the line, cross bat**.

hitting over the top
A shot struck in the air over the mid-distance fielders.

hit wicket
Dismissal created by batsman striking his stumps in the execution of a stroke with his person, his dress or equipment.

Hobbs, Sir John (Jack)
English cricketer considered by many to be the best batsman ever and the first professional to be knighted.

hoick
A cross-batted shot alien to cricket coaching textbooks. *See* **cross bat, text book**.

hole out
Loft an intended boundary stroke to an outfielder.

Hong Kong Sixes
Annual competition for teams of six players held in the Far East.

hook
Leg side stroke behind square played to a ball pitching short of a length.

hostile
Used generally in reference to aggressive and potential injury causing bowling.

how's that? (howzat?)
Appeal to the umpire for a batsman's dismissal, covering all ways of being out. *See* **appeal, umpire**.

hundred
A batsman's landmark score of one hundred runs in an innings. *See* **century, ton**.

hung up his boots
Idiom used in respect of a player who has decided to conclude his career.

Hutton, Sir Leonard
One of England's greatest opening batsmen. Born in Pudsey in 1916 and played for Yorkshire from 1934 to 1955. When he led England against India at Leeds in 1952, he became the first professional to captain England. Played 79 Tests, scoring 6,971 runs at an average of 56.67. Led England to victory over the touring Australians in 1953 to regain Ashes. Knighted in 1956 for his services to the game. Died 1990. *See* **Ashes, Yorkshire CCC**.

hitter

I

ice bath
Ice filled container in which players submerge themselves after play in order to 'warm down' the muscles.

if three can't do it, four won't
Adage which refers to the selectors' decision on the number of seam bowlers to be used in a Test match.

illegal delivery
A ball that contravenes the Laws of cricket.

Imperial Cricket Conference
Forerunner of the International Cricket Council.

in arrears
A team's deficit at the end of an innings.

in close
Close set field of catchers.

inconsistent bounce
See variable bounce.

Incrediball
Rubber ball with a stitched seam used in inter cricket.

India
Full members of the ICC since 1926. The game was introduced to the sub-continent by the British in the late 18th century. The Calcutta Cricket Club was founded in 1792 on the site of Calcutta's current Test ground at Eden Gardens. India were introduced to Test cricket in 1926, the same year that New Zealand and West Indies made the breakthrough. Sunil Gavaskar, a prolific run-machine, led India out of the doldrums in the 1970s. They beat England in an away series in 1971 and again at home in 1972–3 and celebrated their finest hour in 1983 when their great young all-rounder Kapil Dev led them to victory over the West Indies in the World Cup final. *See* Eden Gardens.

indoor cricket
Played in nets on a court and offering a variety of scoring opportunities for batsmen who can take up to seven runs off a single ball. *See* nets.

in-ducker
A delivery that swings into a right-handed batsman. Also known as an inswinger.

infield
Fielders situated close to the striking batsman.

in good nick
To be playing well.

injuries
Players are susceptible to injuries, the most common being bruising and broken fingers (batsmen); groin, hamstring and shoulder strains (bowlers); leg and throwing arm injuries (fielders).

Indian Premier League (IPL)
Indian Cricket League (ICL)

inners

Second pair of gloves worn inside batting
gloves or wicket-keeping gloves.

inner thigh pad

Pad worn inside a player's flannels to protect
upper leg. *See* **flannels**.

innings

The performance of a team's batsmen,
measured ultimately by the aggregate number of
runs scored by the eleven batsmen. First-class
matches consist of four innings, two per side.

innings defeat

Ignominious rout brought about by the losing
side, having batted twice, failing to score
enough runs to make the opposition bat again.

innings run rate

The speed at which runs are scored per innings.

in one's ground

To be behind the batting crease ensuring that
you cannot be run out or stumped.

in-out field

Field setting comprising a balance of close
catchers with a number of defensive positions
on the boundary and necessitated by the need
to take wickets while defending a small total.

inside edge

The edge of the bat nearer the pads when a
batsman takes guard.

inside the circle

Fielders positioned inside the zone established
for limited-overs cricket.

inswinger

A delivery that swings into a right-handed
batsman. *See* **in-ducker**.

inter cricket

Grass roots initiative which bridges the gap
between Kwik cricket and the hard ball game.

International Cricket Council (ICC)

The governing body for world cricket, with
headquarters at Lord's. It comprises ten full
member countries, Australia, Bangladesh,
England, India, New Zealand, Pakistan, South
Africa, Sri Lanka, West Indies and Zimbabwe. On
15 June 1909 representatives of cricket in
England, Australia and South Africa met at Lord's
and founded the Imperial Cricket Conference.
Membership was confined to the governing
bodies of cricket in countries within the British
Commonwealth where Test cricket was played.
India, New Zealand and West Indies were elected
as members on 31 May 1926, Pakistan on 28
July 1952, Sri Lanka on 21 July 1981,
Zimbabwe on 8 July 1992 and Bangladesh on
26 June 2000. South Africa ceased to be a
member of ICC on leaving the British
Commonwealth in May 1961, but was elected as
a Full Member on 10 July 1991. On 7 July
1993, ICC ceased to be administered by MCC
and became an independent organisation with its
own chief executive, the headquarters remaining
at Lord's. In June 2000 Sir Paul Condon, the
former Metropolitan Police Commissioner, was
appointed by the ICC to lead cricket's first
international anti-corruption unit. *See* **MCC**.

ICC Code of Conduct

In September 1999, a new Code of Conduct
applicable to players and team officials was
introduced. ICC match referees are
empowered to 'police' the code. If a breach of
the code is committed, the match referee
holds an investigation and imposes an
appropriate sentence where necessary. *See*
match referee.

inners

ICC Trophy
Played between associate member countries every four years. The winning country gains a place in the next World Cup.

International Panel of Umpires
Comprises two umpires from each of the ten test playing nations and eligible to stand in one-day internationals.

interval
The break for lunch and tea. A 'drinks break' of short duration can also be taken by players during an innings. *See* **drinks break**.

in the air
A lofted shot.

in the box seat
In control of the outcome of the match.

in the channel
A bowler's capacity to deliver the ball on a clearly defined path down the pitch to the striking batsman's discomfort.

in the deep
An area occupied by fielders nearer the boundary edge than the playing square.

in the groove
A bowler delivering the ball with studied rhythm, line and length.

in the hutch
The return of a dismissed batsman to the pavilion.

in the middle
Used to describe the playing area during a match.

in the slot
A ball overpitched, allowing the batsman to drive on the half-volley.

in the V
A striking batsman's ability to play shots into an imaginary 'V' shaped zone between extra cover and mid-wicket.

in the zone
A total concentration of mind and body.

intimidation
Applied to a pace bowler who is prepared to rough up a batsman by contravening the laws governing short-pitched deliveries. *See* **pace bowler**.

Invincibles, The
Donald Bradman's 1948 Australian touring team, so called because they remained unbeaten that summer in England. *See* **Sir Donald Bradman**.

invitation ball
Teasing delivery the purpose of which is to draw the batsman into making a mistake.

Iqbal Stadium
One of the most recent of Pakistan's Test venues in Faisalabad. Staged its first match in 1979.

it's not cricket
Figure of speech indicating unacceptable behaviour. *See* **fair play.**

J

jab
A short-armed stroke played with the minimum of movement and footwork.

jack in the box
A batsman prone to extravagance rather than caution.

Jade Stadium
Test match ground in Christchurch, the headquarters of cricket in New Zealand, surrounded by an abundance of trees and church spires.

jaffa
Delivery of high quality.

jag
Delivery that moves from the off or leg on pitching.

jagged away
Delivery that leaves a batsman, moving from leg to off.

jagged back
Delivery that cuts back into a batsman from the off.

jock-strap
Elasticated support for the box designed to protect the batsman's genitalia. *See* **box.**

joke bowler
An undisciplined, ineffective and irregular bowler.

journeyman
A player of modest ability.

juggle
To fumble the ball before securing a catch.

juice in the pitch
Moisture in the pitch surface making it conducive to seam bowlers.

jute
Fibre from bark of Indian plant sometimes used to make covering for wickets in areas of poor grass growth.

K

kadak
Indian word which, when used in the context of cricket, means the outward display of fighting spirit.

Kanga cricket
Australian forerunner of Kwik cricket.

Karachi National Stadium
Pakistan Test match ground in the bustling city of Karachi, the country's financial capital.

keeping
Abbreviation for wicket-keeping.

keeping a straight bat
Ability to play the bowling in textbook fashion with a perpendicular bat. *See* **text book**.

keep it tight
An instruction to bowlers or the fielding team not to concede runs.

keep low
A delivery of low bounce.

keep the scoreboard ticking
Instruction to the batting side to score runs at regular intervals.

Kensington Oval
West Indian Test match ground in Bridgetown, Barbados. Purchased at public auction in 1914 for £250, it hosted the first ever Test match in the West Indies against England in 1930. Fire destroyed all its wooden stands in 1944.

Kent CCC
The club was established on 1 March 1859. The county was admitted to the County Championship in 1895. The club colours are maroon and white. The badge is a white horse on a red background. Ground: St Lawrence, Canterbury.

Kenya
Emerging cricket nation with a Test playing future possible if development is maintained. First cricket match took place in 1899. Kenya played as part of East Africa in the first ICC Trophy in 1979, but in 1982 they broke away and achieved their own identity. Kenya made world headlines at the 1996 World Cup by defeating the mighty West Indies. They reached the ICC Trophy Final in 1997. *See* **ICC Trophy**.

kidology
To tease, tempt an opponent into making a mistake using cunning and guile.

kill the game
To adopt a negative approach in an effort to avoid losing.

king pair
See golden pair.

Kingsmead
South African Test match ground in Durban. Situated close to the coast, it lends itself well to swing bowling, particularly when the tide comes in and the water table rises. *See* swing.

kit
Any piece of equipment required to play cricket.

knee roll
The horizontal roll of a batting pad at knee level.

knock
An innings.

knocking in
Method employed for hardening the surface of a new cricket bat, performed with old ball or leather-headed hammer.

knockout
Form of competition or tournament in which the loser at each stage is eliminated.

know-how
The gift of natural talent.

knuckle ball
A pace bowler's slower delivery effected by wedging the ball between the fore and middle fingers.

Kookaburra
Australian manufacturer of cricket equipment.

Kwik cricket
Game of cricket for children up to eleven years. Played with plastic stumps and bats and soft non-bruising ball.

Kolpak player
Maros Kolpak, a professional handball player from Slovakia, had a victory in the European Court in 2003, over his right not to be classed a foreigner in the German League. This has led to his name being used to describe the mass influx of cricketers now plying their trade in county cricket. These players come from countries holding trade agreements with the European Union.

L

La Bahadur Shastri Stadium
Batsman-friendly Indian Test match ground at Hyderabad. Originally known as the Fatah Maidan, it was renamed in memory of the former Indian Prime Minister.

lacquer
Finishing treatment applied to a cricket ball.

Lancashire CCC
Formation of the present club was on 12 January 1864. The county was admitted to the official County Championship in 1890. The club colours are red, green and blue. The badge is a red rose. Ground: Old Trafford, Manchester.

lap
Cross batted shot in which a ball pitching on or outside the off stump is played onto the leg side between mid wicket and square leg. *See* **cross bat**.

larup
To hit the ball with great force and venom.

late cut
Wristy shot played late with horizontal bat to send the ball behind square through the slip region.

late / lower order batsman
Occupying a batting position between eight and eleven on the team sheet.

lateral movement
Sideways movement on the ball after pitching.

Laws of Cricket
First compiled in 1744 by 'Noblemen and Gentlemen' who played on London's Artillery Ground. Revisions were made in 1755 and 1774, the latter compiled by a committee of Noblemen and Gentlemen of Kent, Hampshire, Surrey, Sussex, Middlesex and London. The first MCC Code of Laws was approved on 19 May 1835. Since the last War, MCC, the accepted guardian of the Laws, have made four major revisions, the last carried out in 2000.

leading edge
Batsman's mistimed stroke resulting in his striking the ball with the edge of the bat rather than the full blade.

leaking runs
The fielding side's inability to stem the run-flow.

leave
When a bastman deliberately opts not to hit the ball.

leaving the field

This is at the discretion of the umpires and allowed only if a player has been injured or becomes ill during play in the event of which a twelfth man may be used. *See* **twelfth man, umpire**.

left-hander

Also known as cack-hander. Batsman whose right shoulder and right side points towards the bowler as he prepares to receive the ball.

leg before wicket (lbw)

Dismissal achieved when a delivery strikes the batsman's pad, equipment or body which, in the umpire's opinion at the bowler's end, would have gone on to hit the stumps. Covered by Law 36. *See* **umpire**.

leg break

A delivery that spins from leg to off on pitching.

leg bye run(s)

Awarded to the batting side when the ball strikes the batsman's person and the two batsmen run.

leg-cutter

Delivery bowled at pace which moves from leg to off on pitching.

leggie

Leg break bowler.

leg glance

Shot to leg behind square played with closed bat face.

leg glide

See **leg glance**.

leg guards

Protective pads.

leg gully

Close catching fielding position just backward of square on the leg side.

leg side

The whole of the playing area on the side of the pitch on which the striking batsman stands.

legside ring

Defensive cordon of fielders on the leg side.

leg slip

Close catching fielding position behind the leg stump.

leg spin

A leg break bowler's spun movement of the ball off the pitch from leg to off.

leg spinner

A bowler who turns the ball off the pitch from leg to off using wrist and fingers to impart spun energy on the ball.

leg stump

Stump nearest a right-handed batsman's right heel when he takes guard.

leg theory

See **bodyline bowling**.

leg trap

Cordon of close catchers positioned behind the striking batsman on the leg side.

Leicestershire CCC

The formation of the present club was on 25 March 1879. The county was admitted to the

leaving the field

official County Championship in 1895. The club colours are dark green and scarlet. The badge is a gold running fox on a green background. Main ground: Grace Road, Leicester.

length
Point where the ball pitches after delivery by the bowler.

life
A batsman, having survived a possible dismissal, being given another chance. Also refers to the nature of the wicket as having discernible resilience.

lifeless pitch
Playing surface which offers no assistance to the bowlers.

lifter
A sharply-rising delivery.

light meter
Electronic apparatus used by umpires for measuring the quality of light. *See* **umpire**.

limited-over match
One-day match to decide which team can score most runs in the number of overs allocated.

linchpin
Pivotal player around which a team is built.

line
Direction of the ball after delivery by the bowler.

line and length
Prerequisite of all good bowlers to deliver the ball accurately and pitch it at a point giving the batsman least comfort.

line decision
Determination by the umpire when judging a run out or stumping appeal.

linseed oil
Applied to the bat to preserve the willow.

lively wicket
Pitch offering bowlers, seam movement and spin.

loam
Rich soil used in the preparation of pitches.

lob
Delivery of high, looping trajectory.

lofted drive
Driven stroke off the front foot sending the ball high into the outfield.

lollipop
A delivery so off line and length that it invites the batsman to dispatch it for a boundary. *See* **line and length**.

long barrier
Textbook fielding technique whereby the player goes down on one knee and places his body behind the ball to stop it.

long handle
Late-order slogger, sometimes called a 'long handle merchant'.

long hop
Short pitched ball inviting the batsman to score freely off the back foot.

long off
Deep fielder positioned on the off side in the arc between deep extra cover and the boundary edge directly behind the bowler.

long on
Deep fielder positioned on the leg-side in the arc between deep mid-wicket and the boundary edge directly behind the bowler.

Long Room, The
Inner sanctum in the pavilion at Lord's from which MCC members watch cricket. *See* **Lord's, MCC**.

long stop
Fielding position in the deep behind the wicket-keeper.

looked all at sea
Expression implying that the batsman was uncomfortable in the execution of his role at the wicket.

loop
Flighted trajectory employed by a spin bowler.

loose ball
A wayward delivery.

loosener
Gentle delivery, lacking penetration at the beginning of a bowler's stint.

Lord's
The world's most famous ground and home of English cricket. Thomas Lord, a rich wine merchant, found the ground and leased it in his own name. On 31 May 1787, Middlesex played Essex on Lord's ground, Dorset Fields, and the legend began. The ground is owned by MCC and leased to Middlesex and the England and Wales Cricket Board for use as a Test match ground. The current ground is actually the third in the St John's Wood district of London known as 'Lord's' – the two previous ones now being covered by building developments. *See* **Essex CCC, MCC, Middlesex CCC**.

Lord's Taverners
Charitable fund raising organisation formed by actors and entertainers, who share a love of cricket, and so called because they used to meet in the tavern adjacent to Lord's cricket ground.

lost ball
Law 20 says that if a ball in play cannot be found or recovered, any fielder may call 'lost ball'. The ball shall then become dead. When 'lost ball' is called, the batting side are awarded either the runs completed by the batsmen, together with the run in progress, or six runs, whichever is the greater.

lower order
The tail enders in a batting order.

lunch interval
The break at the end of a morning's play.

M

MA Chidabaram Stadium

Indian Test match ground regarded as the spiritual home of cricket in the state of Madras whose fans are reputed to be among the most knowledgeable in the country.

MacLaurin, Lord

Former chairman of the England and Wales Cricket Board and chairman of British-based telecommunications group Vodafone.

maiden century

A batsman's first hundred.

maiden over

An over of six deliveries in which no runs are scored off the bat. Also known as a dry over.

maker's name

The manufacturer's logo on a bat.

mallet

Wooden hammer used to harden the surface of a cricket bat. *See* **knocking in**.

Manhattan

Graph showing side's run-rate with scores arranged in the shape of New York tower blocks. *See* **run rate**.

Mankad(ded)

An extremely rare form of run out whereby the incoming bowler removes the bails of the backing up, non-striking batsman's wicket without releasing the ball and named after the celebrated Indian all-rounder Vinoo Mankad.

man of the match

Player chosen as the best performer at the end of a match.

man of the series

Player chosen as the best performer at the end of a series of matches.

marigolds

Euphemism for a wicket-keeper's gloves.

marker

Small object used to mark the beginning of a bowler's run-up.

marl

Soil mixture of clay and lime used as a fertiliser in the preparation of pitches.

Marylebone Cricket Club, The (MCC)

Evolved out of the old White Conduit Club in 1787 when Thomas Lord opened his first ground in Dorset Fields. The private member's club revised the laws in 1787 and gradually took responsibility for cricket throughout the world. It relinquished control of the game in

the United Kingdom in 1968 and the International Cricket Council established its own secretariat in 1993. MCC purchased Lord's cricket ground in 1866 for £18,333 6s 9d. Middlesex County Cricket Club first played there in 1877 and have been tenants ever since. MCC's first centenary was celebrated by the purchase of Henderson's Nursery (hence Nursery End). MCC still owns Lord's and is the guardian of the Laws. It describes its modern role as a 'private club with a public function' and attempts to support cricket all over the world. *See* **International Cricket Council, Lord's, Middlesex CCC**.

match abandoned
Match terminated prematurely. *See* **abandoned**.

match conceded
Game in which the result is forfeited.

match fixing
Conspiracy to arrange the result of a match for monetary gain.

match plan
See **strategy**.

match referee
Armchair official responsible for adjudicating fair play.

match sponsor
Person or company giving financial backing to a particular match.

maximum
A score of six runs from a single stroke, signalled by the umpire raising both hands above his head.

M. Chinnaswarmy Stadium
Indian Test match venue in Bangalore and named after a former president of the Indian Cricket Board.

meat and drink
See **bread and butter**.

meat of the bat
Area of a cricket bat from which the most power is generated. *See* **sweet-spot**.

medals
Colourful term used to describe the bruises inflicted on a batsman through being struck by the ball.

medium pace
Bowling in the speed range 60-75 mph.

Melbourne Cricket Ground
Regarded as Australia's premier sporting venue with a capacity of 97,000. The first ever test match was held at the MCG in 1877. It also hosts Aussie rules, soccer, Rugby Union and Rugby League and was the centrepiece of the 1956 Olympic Games.

mental disintegration
Loss of composure by a player, usually as a result of frustration.

Mexican wave
Appreciative synchronised raising of arms by spectators around the ground.

Michelle
Rhyming slang (Michelle Pfeiffer) for taking five wickets in a innings.

match abandoned

middle and leg

Batsman's guard when positioning his bat in the block-hole between middle and leg stumps, often called 'two legs' by batsmen seeking a guard from umpires.

middle and off

Batsman's guard when positioning his bat in the block-hole between off stump and middle stump.

middled the ball

Perfect timing with the ball dispatched from the meat of the bat.

middle order

Numbers four to seven in the batting line-up.

middle practice

Coaching session conducted on the pitch to simulate match conditions.

Middlesex CCC

The present club was established on 2 February 1864. The county was admitted to the official County Championship in 1890. The club colours are blue. The badge is three seaxes. Ground: Lord's, London.

middle stump

Stump erected between off stump and leg stump.

mid-off

Fielding position on the off side between extra-cover and the bowler.

mid-on

Fielding position on the leg side between mid-wicket and the bowler.

mid-wicket

Fielding position on the leg side between square leg and mid on.

milk

To score easy runs and feed off the bowling.

military medium

A brisk but not outstandingly quick bowler.

minefield

See cabbage patch.

minor counties

The Minor Counties Cricket Association was formed in Birmingham in 1895 to provide competition for non first class counties and the second elevens of first class counties. A separate competition for the latter was established in 1959. The association has representatives on the ECB. Durham, now one of the eighteen first-class championship counties, were Minor Counties champions on several occasions before their elevation. *See* Durham CCC.

minor cricketing nations

Canada, Fiji, Kenya, Holland and Scotland do not play Test cricket but compete for a place in the World Cup one-day tournament.

miscue

A poorly executed stroke in which the ball leaves the bat in a direction not intended.

misfield

A ball not fielded cleanly.

moisture

Dampness in a pitch offering conditions ideal for seam bowling.

moon shot

Aggressive stroke in which the ball is dispatched in the air to the leg side boundary.

movement
When the ball changes direction in flight or off the pitch when delivered by a bowler

movement in the air
A bowler's capacity to swing the ball in the atmosphere, either outswing with the ball moving from leg to off in the air, or inswing with the ball travelling in the reverse direction.

movement off the seam
Delivery that changes direction off the stitched seam of the ball when hitting the pitch.

mullygrubber
Australian for a poor delivery which bounces at least twice before reaching the batsman.

Multan Cricket Stadium
East Pakistan Test match ground in Punjab which hosted the final of the inaugural Asian Test Championship in 2001.

movement

N

National Academy

Initiative created by the majority of Test playing nations to nurture the development of talented young cricketers.

National Cricket League

Sponsored one-day competition. *See* Norwich Union.

natural game

To play in the manner to which a batsman is accustomed rather than adopt a style foreign to his nature.

NatWest Trophy

Formerly English cricket's premier one-day competition, ending with a traditional showpiece final and finale to the season at Lord's. Now called the Cheltenham & Gloucester Trophy after sponsor's National Westminster Bank transferred its financial support to the NatWest one-day series between England and summer tourists.

negative bowling

Bowling usually aimed down the batsman's leg side which restricts scoring options.

Nelsons

Score of 111 runs (or when all three figures in the score are the same, i.e. 222, 333 and so forth), considered to be an unlucky number, especially in Australia, and often signalled by the umpire at the bowling end of the wicket hopping three times on one leg . Origin of this term is based on the erroneous notion that Admiral Nelson had one eye, one arm, and one testicle.

nervous nineties

Pressure felt by the batsman as he approaches a score of a hundred and the signal for extra effort by the bowlers.

net

Session of practice for a batsman or bowler.

Netherlands, The

Cricket in Holland began in 1855 when South African students at Utrecht University introduced the game, but it was another twenty years before cricket really became established. By the 1880s there were dozens of club sides. The Netherlands beat the touring Australians in 1964. Reached the ICC Trophy final in 1986, losing narrowly to Zimbabwe. The Zimbabweans beat them again in the 1990 final. They qualified for the 1996 World Cup on the strength of coming third in the ICC Trophy in 1994, but lost all their five matches on the Indian sub-continent.

net run rate

The difference between a team's acumulative run rate and the combined acummulative run rate of its opponents, used in tournaments and league systems.

nets
Enclosed area of netting where players practise batting or bowling on an artificial or grass pitch inside a covered building or in the open air.

never run on a misfield
Adage relating to the risk of being run out after a fielder has fumbled the ball.

new ball
Unused cricket ball given to the captain of the fielding team at the start of an innings. In an English championship match, the captain of the fielding side has the choice of taking a new ball after 80 overs have been bowled with the old one.

new-ball bowler
A bowler given the responsibility of using the new ball.

Newlands
One of the most picturesque of South Africa's Test match grounds in Cape Town and characterised by the surrounding rows of oak trees which were planted in 1902.

New Wanderers Stadium
South African Test match ground in Johannesburg.

New Zealand
Full members of the ICC since 1926. A three-day match between Otago and Canterbury provinces at Dunedin in 1864 is considered the starting point for first-class cricket there.

Despite their promotion to Test status in 1926, their first fifty years of Test cricket was played for little reward. But directly after World War II the Kiwis produced their first world-class batsman, Bert Sutcliffe. Later came another, John Reid, and the bowler Sir Richard Hadlee, the greatest cricketer New Zealand has produced, as Test and one-day results began to improve dramatically.

Niaz Stadium
Pakistan Test match ground at Hyderabad in the southern province of Sindh.

nibble
To fish for the ball with the bat without making contact. *See* **fishing**.

nick
To edge a chance to the wicket-keeper or close infielders.

niggle
A slight and irritating injury.

night-watchman
Late order batsman promoted to higher batting position late in the day in the hope he can absorb time without losing a wicket to the scheduled end of play.

nips away
Delivery that hurries off the pitch from leg to off.

nips back
Delivery that hurries off the pitch from off towards leg.

no ball
An illegal delivery that contravenes Law 24.

nets

no-decision signal

Given by the third umpire in cases where a decision is inconclusive due to the failure of the television monitoring equipment. *See* **third umpire**.

non-striker

Batsman at the bowler's end not facing the next delivery.

no result

A match incompleted because of bad weather or other factors.

Northamptonshire CCC

Formation of the present club was on 31 July, 1878. The county was admitted to the official County Championship in 1905. The club colours are maroon. The badge is a Tudor rose. Ground: County Ground, Northampton.

Norwich Union

Old established insurance company and sponsors of the one-day national cricket league.

not out

The end of an individual innings in which the batsman remains undefeated.

Nottinghamshire CCC

The present club was established in the spring of 1841. The county was admitted to the official County Championship in 1890. The club colours are green and gold. The badge is a leaping stag. Ground: Trent Bridge, Nottingham.

npower

British electricity supplier and sponsor of England's home Test series.

nudge

A push stroke played with the minimum of backlift and power.

nurdle

Similar to a nudge but played with deliberate method to manoeuvre the ball for runs through a close-set cordon of fielders behind square on the off or leg sides.

nursery end

Bowling end at Lord's cricket ground, on the far side from the pavillion. *See* **Marylebone Cricket Club**.

nutmeg

A ball striking the wickets after passing through the legs of the batsman.

O

obstructing the field
See obstruction.

obstruction
Either batsman is given out 'obstructing the field' if he wilfully obstructs or distracts the opposing side by word or action. This offence is governed by Law 37.

occupation of the crease
The duration of a batsman's innings.

off break
Delivery that spins from off to leg on pitching.

off cutter
Delivery bowled at pace that cuts into the batsman from the off after hitting the pitch.

off drive
Stroke played off the front foot with a full swing of the bat that dispatches the ball through the mid-off region.

offer the light
Umpires may give batsmen the chance to interrupt their innings and leave the middle if they believe poor light impairs their vision.

officials
Two umpires are used, one standing behind the bowler's wicket and the other at square leg. They alternate after each over. In some major matches a third umpire is employed, adjudicating line decisions from the pavilion, and a match referee is on duty. *See* **match referee, third umpire**.

off side
The side of the ground the batsman faces when adopting his stance to face a bowler. *See* **stance**.

offside ring
Cordon of fielders between slip and mid-off.

off stump
Stump nearest the wicket-keeper's right hand when standing up to a right handed batsman.

off the mark
First run of a batsman's innings.

off the pad
Ricochet off the leg guards.

Old Father Time
The weather vane that surmounts the stand at Lord's.

Old Trafford
Manchester's Test match ground and one of the world's most famous cricketing venues. Record gate was 78,617 for a Roses match (Lancashire v Yorkshire) in 1926. The home of Lancashire since 1857, the year the ground was opened. Built on

level, sandy soil, the ground suffered damage during World War II when commandeered by the army for resting soldiers on their return from Dunkirk. *See* **Lancashire CCC**.

on a roll
Sequence of match-winning performances.

on drive
Stroke off the front foot through the mid-on region.

one-day international
Limited-overs match between two countries.

one-day match
A match of limited-overs duration played in one day.

one-day specialist
Individual or team adept at performing well in limited-overs matches.

one leg
A leg stump guard. *See* **taking guard.**

one short
Umpire's signal when a batsman has not completed a full run.

on side
The area of the ground behind a batsman when addressing the next delivery.

on strike
Batsman set to play the next ball.

on the back foot
Individual or team thrust into defensive mode by an individual or side on top of their game.

on the up
Making ground after barren batting patch. Also

driving a ball that is rising from a good length.

open action
Chest-on action at a bowler's point of delivery.

openers
See **opening pair**.

opening batsman
Batsman filling the number one or two positions at the start of an innings.

open the shoulders
Point at which a batsman decides to play more aggressive shots.

opening pair
Opening batting partnership at the start of an innings. Can also refer to the two bowlers who start the innings.

opening the face of the bat
Ball struck with the full face of the blade thrust at the oncoming ball.

open stance
When a batsman opens his front foot to the leg side and presents more of his chest to the bowler.

opening bowler(s)
The first and second bowler used at the start of an innings.

orthodox
Batsman or bowler whose style follows closely the traditional teachings of the coaching manuals and textbooks.

orthodox spinner
Finger spinner as opposed to wrist spinner.

out
Dismissed.

out-dipper
Australian equivalent of an outswinger.

outer
Australian for the public viewing area.

outfield
Open acres between the inner rim of fielders and the boundary rope.

outfielder
A player not in a close catching position.

outfit
Slang for a team.

out of his ground
Batsman trapped down the pitch, out of his crease, and about to be stumped by the wicket-keeper. Can also apply to being run out. *See* **stumped**.

outside edge
Edge of the bat further from the pads during a batsman's stance.

outswinger
Ball moving in flight from leg to off when delivered by a bowler. Known as an out-dipper in Australia.

Oval (Kennington), The AMP
Famous English Test match ground south of the River Thames in London. Home of Surrey County Cricket Club since 1845, the year in which William Baker secured the lease of a market garden from the Duchy of Cornwall. Len Hutton scored a then world record 364 in 1938. In 1998 Sri Lankan off-spin bowler Muttiah Muralitharan took sixteen wickets in a Test against England. Many other sports have been staged on the ground, including association football, athletics and rugby. It staged the first ever Test on home soil between England and Australia in September 1880 and tradition since has dictated that the final Test of a summer series is held on this ground. *See* **Surrey CCC**.

over(s)
Six legitimate deliveries from a bowler constitute one over. Overs are bowled alternately from each end of the pitch.

overarm
Method employed for bowling in the modern game. It was legalised in 1864, a product of roundarm bowling which had been in fashion since that form of delivery was legalised in 1835.

over-pitch(ed)
Delivery pitched too far up to the batsman, allowing him a chance to score easy runs.

over rate
The tempo at which overs are bowled. A minimum of 104 overs must be bowled on the first three days of an English championship match with a minimum of 80, plus one hour, stipulated for the final day's play and 90 per day in Test matches.

overseas player
Team member drafted in from abroad.

overs in hand
The overs still to be bowled when a target has been reached by the team batting second.

over the wicket
The route a right-handed bowler takes to arrive at the stumps at the left side of the umpire standing at the non-striking end.

overthrows
Throw-in that defeats wicket-keeper or fielder guarding the stumps and travels on for overthrown runs.

P

pace
Fast bowling.

pace attack
Team's fast bowling armoury.

pace bowler
Fast bowler. Also known as a paceman.

paceman
See pace bowler.

Packer, Kerry
Australian media mogul who in 1977 signed up many of the world's top players to play a series of one-day and Test matches in Australia. He established World Series Cricket following his rebuff by the Australian Board of Control over the rights to screen cricket in Australia on Channel 9 television, which he owned. The ICC ruled that no player who had joined WSC would be eligible for Test cricket, but Packer challenged that ruling in the High Court in London and won a conclusive victory.

pad-bat catch
A dismissal by which the ball is deflected off the pad then bat to a fielder.

padded away
To use pads rather than bat to play the ball away from the stumps.

paddle stroke
A sweep shot.

pads
Leg protection for batsmen and wicket-keepers

pad up
Refers to a batsman offering no shot, preferring to use his front pad to return the ball back in the direction of the bowler. Also to strap on pads in preparation to bat.

paidal
Indian for poor bowling.

pair, a
Two noughts in two innings of the same match.

Pakistan
Admitted as a member of the ICC in July, 1952 and played its first Test, against India, in 1952–3 season. Within five years they had achieved Test victories over England, Australia, New Zealand and India. *See* Quaid-E-Azam Trophy.

parry
A fielders skilful deflection of the ball to another player to make the catch.

partnership
A stand between two batsmen. Also the combination of two bowlers. *See* stand.

patron
Australian for a spectator.

pavilion
The word first occurred in English, probably in the 12th century as pavilun, from the Old French pavilloun, meaning a canopied structure and derived from the Latin papilio. A building that accommodates cricketers during matches.

pavilion end
Part of the ground nearest the pavilion.

pearler
Exclamation of appreciation in respect of a ball of exceptional quality.

pea roller
See shooter.

peg
Slang for a stump.

pelting
Bowling action, resembling chucking, used in soft ball cricket throughout the Caribbean.

penalty runs
Awarded for transgression of the rules and covered under Section 18 of the Laws of Cricket.

penetrative bowling
Difficult bowling in which the batsmen perish or struggle to survive.

pick
Batsman's ability to read correctly a bowler's disguised delivery.

picked the gap(s)
Batsman's ability to puncture the field placings with his shots.

pick-up
Lifting of the bat in preparation for a shot.

pierced the field
See picked the gap.

pie thrower
Colourful Australian term for a bowler of poor quality.

pinch-hitter/hitting
Attacking batsman promoted in the batting order to give the start of an innings run-making impetus.

pitch
The strip of mown turf between the two sets of stumps.

pitched short
A ball delivered short of a length.

pitched up
A delivery of full length.

pitch report
Media analysis of the condition of the playing surface prior to a match.

plank
Uncomplimentary description of a poor quality bat.

play
Umpire's call to start a game.

played across the line
A shot in which the batsman has played across the line of the oncoming delivery.

played on
A batsman plays the ball off his bat onto his stumps to be dismissed 'bowled'.

players, the
A match is played between two sides, each of eleven players, one of whom shall be captain.

player's conduct
In the event of a player failing to comply with instructions by an umpire, or criticising by word or action the decisions of an umpire, or generally behaving in a manner which might bring the game into disrepute, the umpire concerned shall in the first place report the matter to the other umpire and to the player's captain, and instruct the latter to take action.

playing back
Playing the ball off the back foot.

playing forward
Playing the ball off the front foot.

playing for your average
Selfish gesture in which the batsman puts his need for runs ahead of the aims of his side.

playing sessions
A day's play in a first-class match consists of three sessions; morning, afternoon, and evening.

playing surface
The ground on which the match is played inside the boundary rope.

play yourself in
Advice to bat conservatively early in an innings in order to assess the pace of the wicket.

plumb
To be given out plumb leg before wicket is to suffer a dismissal so obvious there is no cause for argument.

plumb wicket
A pitch of true bounce and pace.

point
Close fielding position square with the wicket on the off side between gully and cover point.

Poms
An Australian expression for English cricketers (or the English in general), used freely whenever England meet Australia in an Ashes series.

popping crease
The white line on which the batsman takes guard and rests his bat before addressing the ball.

post a score
To set the opposition a target.

postponed
When a match cannot be played at its set time but is rescheduled for another time or date.

pouch
To take a catch cleanly.

powder puff team
Side which lacks resolve and crumbles easily in the face of adversity.

power cricket
Limited overs match played indoors and

divided into four 15-over innings with each side batting alternately. A maximum of five overs per bowler and three substitutions allowed per innings.

preparation and maintenance of the playing area
Work carried out by the groundsman and his staff before or after the start of play.

pressure
Nervous tension brought about by the fear of failure which some players handle more effectively than others.

Primary Club, The
Membership qualification depends on a person's ability to prove that he has had the misfortune to be dismissed first ball for a golden duck. This prestigious organisation runs a fixture list of matches to raise funds for charity. *See* duck.

professional
Status of a paid player.

Professional Cricketers' Association (PCA)
Was formed in 1967 (as the Cricketers' Association) to represent the first-class county staffs, and to promote and protect professional players' interests. In the 1970s, it established pension schemes and a minimum wage. In 1995 David Graveney became general secretary and its first full-time employee. In 1998 he became chief executive. Today it raises revenue and funds to provide improved benefits for players during and after their careers.

protective gear
Essential equipment used by batsmen, wicket-keepers and close catchers to safeguard parts of their body from injury.

Proteas
South African national team name.

pudding
Pitch with a benign surface offering little assistance to batsmen or bowlers.

pull shot
A shot played to a short delivery off the back foot in which the ball travels between mid-on and square leg.

Punjab Cricket Association Stadium
The most recent and one of the largest of India's nineteen Test match grounds at Mohali just outside the city of Chandigarh and renowned for its bowler-friendly wicket.

purchase
The amount of spin imparted on a ball either by the bowler or off the pitch.

pushed back into crease
Batsman forced onto the back foot to defend his wicket.

put the brakes on
To adopt a defensive field and line of bowling in order to stem the flow of runs.

put your sweater on
Captain's instruction to a bowler indicating that he is taking him out of the attack.

pyjama cricket
One-day limited-overs cricket played in coloured clothing.

Q

quack
Fun term for scoring no runs – i.e. being out for a duck.

Quaid-E-Azam Trophy
National championship of Pakistan was inaugurated in 1953–4. Major breeding ground for players hoping to make the Test side. Bahawalpur were prominent first winners of the trophy with Hanif Mohammed, one of Pakistan's best ever cricketers instrumental in that success with two centuries. He made the highest individual first-class score of 499, while batting for Karachi against Bahawalpur in 1958–9. His record lasted until 1994 when broken by West Indies batsman Brian Lara, playing for Warwickshire against Durham.

Queensland
Australian state side. When the Australian Board of Control first met in May 1905, Queensland were admitted almost immediately.

Queen's Park Oval
The largest of the five West Indian Test grounds with a capacity of 25,000, the Port of Spain, Trinidad, venue is also regarded as the most attractive, the northern hills providing a breathtaking backdrop.

Queen's Sports Club
Test match ground in Bulawayo, Zimbabwe, famous for the lilac jacaranda trees that ring one side of the ground.

quick bowlers' club
A misnomer based on the notion that a fast bowler will refrain from intimidatory bowling against his opposite number when he is at the batting crease. Also known as Fast Bowlers' Union.

quick delivery
Fast ball.

quickie
A fast bowler. *See* **pace bowler**.

quicksilver
Used to describe a player with extreme agility.

quick single
Sharply taken 'stolen' run to defeat close set field placings.

quixotic innings
Performance of a batsman who unselfishly neglects his own interests in favour of his playing partner or the team in general.

R

rabbit
Unflattering title given to a poor batsman, who is soon dismissed and on his way back to the hutch. *See* **in the hutch, tail-ender, ferret**.

raging turner
A pitch taking prodigious spin.

rain break
Unscheduled stoppage for bad weather.

rain stopped play
Description of unscheduled stoppage caused by rain.

raised the finger
Umpire's hand movement to signal batsman's dismissal.

rattled
To be unsettled by the opposition's attacking play.

Rawalpindi Cricket Stadium
Compact Pakistan Test match ground perched on the edge of the city and only three miles from the capital of Islamabad.

Reader
Proprietary English brand of cricket ball.

reading the delivery
See **pick**.

rearguard action
A team's fight back after initial failure.

rebel tour
Unofficial matches by visiting teams against South Africa when that country was excluded from international sport due to apartheid.

records
Figures kept for posterity to analyse individual or collective match statistics. Scorers belong to the Association of Cricket Umpires and Scorers.

red light
Illuminated signal given by the third umpire from the pavilion to signal that a batsman has been dismissed.

red zone
Coloured electronic strip projected on television to examine the accuracy of an umpire's lbw adjudication.

regulation catch
A simple catching opportunity.

relay fielding
Technique of retrieving the ball with one player stopping it and another making the return throw.

replacement ball
Brought into use when the existing ball has been damaged or lost and must be of similar condition.

reply
The score in response by the side batting second.

retired hurt
If the umpires are satisfied that a player has been injured or is unwell when batting or fielding, they will allow a substitute fielder or a runner for the unfit batsman.

return catch
To hit the ball in the air straight back to the bowler.

return crease
Marks the lateral limits of the bowler's territory, so marked to prevent him from bowling at too acute an angle.

reverse order
Captain's decision to change the batting order so that the tail-enders appear before the openers and middle-order. *See* **middle order, openers, tail enders**.

reverse sweep
Unorthodox stroke in which the batsman reverses his shot and sweeps to the third man boundary rather than the long leg area. The bat is swung in an horizontal arc from leg to off. Product of limited-overs cricket when quick runs are necessary to accelerate the score and defeat a cleverly set field.

reverse swing
Phenomenon created with an aged ball that has been weighted on one side by sweat and grime, thus creating rapid movement in the air.

Get the ball to move as late as possible in its flight; this could be assisted by holding it across the seam so as to scuff it up more quickly (quite legal)

rib tickler
Short delivery that rises to strike a batsman in the rib cage.

Richards, Sir Vivian
Flamboyant West Indian cricketer who received an honorary knighthood in 2000 following a 121 Test match career during which he scored 8,540 runs.

rides the ball
Batsman's ability to get over a sharply rising short delivery.

rising delivery
A ball which climbs steeply off the pitch towards the batsman's upper body.

ripsnorter
Devastating shock ball delivered with exceptional pace or spin to surprise the batsman.

Riverside Ground
The most recent of England's seven Test match venues on the banks of the River Wear at Chester-Le-Street and home of Durham CCC.

road
Benign pitch, giving the bowler no assistance, but every encouragement to the batsman.

roll the fingers over
A pace bowler's method of disguising a slower delivery.

rookie
Newcomer to the side.

rope
See **boundary**.

Roses match
County match between Lancashire, whose emblem is a red rose, and Yorkshire, whose badge sports a white rose.

rotating the strike
Clever tactic employed by batsmen to steal quick runs so that the bowling attack and the fielding side are given little time to settle with the constant change of personnel on strike. *See* bowling attack.

rough
Scuffed-up surface of pitch offering purchase to spin bowlers accurate enough to plant a spinning delivery in that area.

rough up
To intimidate a batsman with short-pitched bowling.

roundarm bowling
Technique with the delivery arm at an angle of almost forty-five degrees and used primarily by leg spinners.

round robin
Method of competition requiring all teams to play one another.

round the wicket
Opposite to over the wicket, the right-handed bowler passing the stumps in his delivery stride with the umpire and stumps on his left.

R. Premadasa Stadium
Sri Lankan Test match ground, named after a former president of the country, and located in the centre of Colombo's commercial district.

rubber
Full programme of matches in a series, e.g. Test rubber; the deciding match in a series in which both sides start with an equal number of wins gained.

run
Scored when the ball is struck and the batsmen exchange ends, or when a no-ball or wide are called by the umpire.

run chase
A team's attempt to achieve a total set by the opposition to win.

run it away
Shot played with an open faced bat guiding the ball behind square on the off side.

run machine
A prolific run scorer.

run-maker
A batsman skilled at compiling runs.

runner
Substitute runner for an injured batsman.

running on the pitch
Trespass by bowlers or fielders on the playing surface of the pitch to gain unfair advantage, often carried out in an attempt to scuff up the strip for the bowlers' benefit.

run out
Mode of dismissal for a batsman caught out of his ground when running between the wickets.

run out ruler
Television device for measuring how far the batsman is out of his crease in a run out decision.

run rate
The tempo at which runs are scored by an

Roses match

individual or side. Particularly relevant to the limited-overs game. *See* **batting rate**.

run scorer
Batsman who scores a run(s).

runs per over
The average number of runs made per over during a bowler's stint or in a side's completed innings.

runs to win
The number of runs required to secure victory.

run the bat in
To slide the bat along the ground over the batting crease in order to make one's ground when taking a run.

run-up
Bowler's journey to the point of delivery.

S

Sabina Park
West Indian Test match ground. Set in the driest part of the Jamaican capital of Kingston, it has the rare distinction of having a Test match (West Indies v England in 1998) abandoned on the opening day due to the dangerous nature of the pitch.

safe hands
Used in relation to a competent and reliable catcher of the ball.

salmon
Australian for an agile fielder.

sandshoe crusher
Term originated by former Australian Test fast bowler Jeff Thomson to describe his yorker.

Sardar Patel Stadium
Indian Test match ground situated on the banks of the Sabarmati River at Ahmedabad.

saving the four
Defensive minded option designed to make the prevention of boundaries more important than the saving of singles.

saving the one / single
Attacking option designed to give the saving of singles priority over the need to prevent boundaries and keep a superior batsman off strike.

sawdust filling
Traditional method for making rain-affected bowlers' footholds more adhesive. *See* foot hold.

scalping
A largely Australian idiom which reflects the illegal action of a bowler intentionally trying to hit the batsman on the head.

score(r)
The total runs scored at any given time; person responsible for logging the runs scored in a scorebook.

scoreboard
The public board on which runs are displayed.

scorecard
The printed document issued to spectators from which they can identify the players selected for the match and record the match statistics as they unfold.

scrambled seam
A pace bowler's delivery with the seam at an angle.

scuff
To disturb the playing surface.

scum
Australian for a score of 36 runs.

scythe
Big swipe at the ball by a batsman without using his feet.

seam
The raised, stitched surface of a cricket ball.

seam bowler
A bowler who uses the seam on the ball to achieve sideways movement off the pitch.

seamer
See seam bowler.

seamer's paradise
Pitch and atmospheric conditions conducive to seam bowling.

seam-up
Bowler who places the ball in a vertical hold between his fingers to achieve sideways movement with his delivery.

season
The period of the year in which cricket is played.

second eleven
The second-string team.

second innings
The second 'dig' in a first-class match.

second slip
The slip catcher positioned immediately to the right of first slip to a right-handed batsman.

seeing it like a football
When a batsman is picking up the line and length of the bowling early enough to play his shots.

selectors
The panel chosen to pick the team.

sells his wicket
Batsman's capacity for giving his wicket away.

send back
A batsman's order to his partner to return to the crease when attempting a risky run.

series
A set of matches played between two Test sides.

sessions
The periods of play in a day: morning, afternoon, evening.

setting the field
The deployment of fielders to any of 24 recognised positions is determined by the captain and dependent on a variety of factors, including the condition of the playing surface and the nature of the bowling attack. (See pages 94–5)

shape
Bowler's ability to impart energy on the ball to achieve movement.

shed, the
Australian for the dressing room.

sheet anchor
Australian for a reliable batsman.

shepherd the tail
Recognised batsman's tactic of taking the strike to protect the lower order batting line-up through the closing stages of an innings.

shine (on the ball)
Rubbing the surface to achieve swing in the air with a delivery.

shirt-front
Benign playing surface.

shirt numbers
Numerals on the back of a cricket shirt to denote the player's identity in a limited-overs match.

shock bowler
Bowler fast enough to discomfort batsman.

shooter
Delivery that scurries along the ground without bouncing after pitching. Also known as a pea roller. More usually, a daisy cutter.

short
Fielding position close to the striking batsman.

short barrier
Fielding technique using a stooped stance and positioning the feet in order to stop a low struck ball.

short forward square
Perilous fielding position close to batsman on leg side.

short leg
Close fielding position on the leg side, in front or behind square.

short leg gully
Close catching fielding position at an angle of 45 degrees behind the batsman.

short of a length
Delivery pitching well short of the batsman.

short pitched
See short of a length.

short run
Run not completed, often known as 'one short'.

short third man
See third man.

short time in the middle
An innings of short duration.

shot
A batting stroke.

shot selection
Batsman's ability to choose the stroke he wants to play and ultimately the direction of the ball.

shot shy
Refers to a batsman who abandons all aggressive instincts and is only prepared to defend.

shoulder
Part of the bat between handle and blade.

shoulder arms
Withdrawal of bat from the path of the oncoming ball by the striking batsman.

shout
Appeal to the umpire for batsman's dismissal.

show the maker's name

Defensive stroke in which the batsman has presented the full face of the bat, which display's the manufacturer's logo, to the oncoming ball.

shut up shop

A batsman's defensive mode in order to protect his wicket.

shy

Speculative throw of the ball at the stumps in a run out attempt.

side

Alternative for team.

sidelined

Unable to participate due to injury or suspension.

sighter

A ball left by a batsman early in his innings to enable him to judge the pace and line of the bowling.

sight-screen

A large screen erected on the boundary edge to give the batsman a better sighting of the ball when it leaves the bowler's hand. A black screen is used behind the bowler's arm in day-night matches when a white ball is used.

signals

Hand signals used by umpires.

signature shot

See trademark stroke.

silly mid-off

Close catching position in front of the striking batsman on the off side.

silly mid-on

Close catching position in front of the striking batsman on the leg side.

silly point

Close catching position square with the striking batsman on the off-side.

single

One run.

Sinhalese Sports Club Ground

Test match venue in Colombo formerly known as Maitland Place and the headquarters of Sri Lankan cricket.

sitter

An easy catch.

six

A shot for six runs that carries beyond the boundary rope without bouncing.

six stitcher

Australian for a cricket ball. *See* tomato.

skiddy wicket

A pitch where the ball keeps low.

skied

An unintentional aerial shot.

skipper

The team's captain.

skittled out

To be bowled out cheaply.

skulled

To be struck on the head by a bouncer.

Sky Track
Television graphic used to assist commentators to decide whether the ball would have hit the stumps after striking the batsman on the pads in a leg before wicket appeal.

sledging
Remark(s) by the fielding side designed to intimidate a batsman.

slice
To play across the line with an open-faced bat.

slider
A spin bowler's delivery that goes straight on without turning after pitching.

slip(s)
The close catching position next to the wicket-keeper for taking edged snicks.

slip cordon
The arc of close catchers deployed on the right of a wicket-keeper to a right-handed batsman.

slipper
Euphemism for a fielder positioned in the slip cordon.

slog
Aggressive stroke executed with little or no regard to textbook coaching technique. *See* **textbook**.

slog sweep
A deliberately lofted sweep down to deep mid wicket.

slower ball
Delivery held back by the bowler to deceive batsman into playing a shot early.

slower delivery
See **slower ball**.

sluggish pitch
Playing surface offering no pace for quick bowlers.

snaffle
To seize an unlikely catch.

snick(ed)
Ball edged by batsman.

snickometer
Television aid developed to determine whether the ball touched bat, glove, pads or body before carrying for a catch.

Sobers, Sir Garfield
Born 1936. Widely regarded as the finest all rounder of modern cricket: received an honorary knighthood in 1975 following a 93 Test match career for the West Indies during which he scored 8,032 runs and took 235 wickets with a mixture of orthodox left arm spin, wrist spin and medium quick bowling.

soft bat
See **soft hands**.

soft hands
Defensive stroke played with a loose-handed grip on the bat to foil close catchers. *See* **hard bat**.

sold
Euphemism for throwing a match.

Somerset CCC
Formation of the present club was on 18 August 1875. The county was admitted to the

official County Championship in 1891. The club colours are black, white and maroon. The badge is the Somerset dragon. Ground: St James Road, Taunton.

South Africa

Full members of the ICC since 1909. British soldiers stationed in South Africa are credited with having introduced cricket there around the beginning of the 19th century. Test cricket began in 1888–9 when England achieved two Test victories at Port Elizabeth. The South African government's apartheid policy led to South Africa's isolation from Test cricket from 1968 until their re-introduction to official international circles at the 1992 World Cup. Their isolation years denied the cricket world an opportunity to watch world-class players Graeme Pollock, Barry Richards, Mike Procter, Clive Rice and Eddie Barlow, but since returning to the Test stage Allan Donald, Jacques Kallis, Daryll Cullinan, Shaun Pollock and Jonty Rhodes have compensated for the lack of opportunity given their predecessors with some performances to challenge Australia's might.

speed gun
Electronic equipment for measuring the pace of a bowler's delivery.

speed merchant
Fast bowler.

spell
Bowling stint.

spiggot
The narrow stem at the end of the bails which rests on the stumps.

spilled chance
A missed catch.

spinner
Bowler who spins the ball.

spinner's paradise
Pitch conditions perfect for a spin bowler.

Spirit of Cricket
Notional rule acknowledging respect for the game's traditional values of fair play. Preamble to the Laws of the game reads: 'Cricket is a game that owes much of its unique appeal to the fact that it should be played not only within its Laws, but also within the Spirit of the Game. Any action which is seen to abuse this spirit causes injury to the game itself. The major responsibility for ensuring the spirit of fair play rests with the captains.'

spitting delivery
A sharply rising ball causing the batsman discomfort.

splice
The v-shaped junction of a bat where the handle dovetails into the blade.

sponsors
Now integral to the finances of the modern game. Companies prepared to support the game by underwriting a player, team or competition, thus promoting their business image in the public esteem.

spooned a catch
Easily offered, gentle catching chance to a fielder.

sporting declaration
Decision taken to ensure a positive result to a match with both sides having a chance of winning.

springs
Indian rubber shock absorbers inserted into the handle of the bat, giving it more feel.

square
The closely mown area from which pitches are prepared. Also defines a position at right angles to the wicket-to-wicket playing strip on off or leg side. *See* **Block.**

square cut
Wristy stroke played square of the wicket on the off side with a horizontal bat.

square drive
Attacking stroke played square of the wicket through the off side.

squared-up
Delivery that hurries a batsman into protecting his stumps in a chest-on position.

square leg
Fielding position at right angles to the striking batsman on the leg side.

square leg umpire
The position on the leg side at right angles to the striking batsman occupied by one of the two umpires.

square of the wicket
A position at right angles to the pitch on the off or leg sides.

Sri Lanka
Full members of the ICC since July 1981. They played their first Test against the touring England team the following February. The first cricket club in the then Ceylon was formed in 1832. The Ceylon Cricket Association was founded in 1922

and an MCC tour team visited in 1927. Sri Lanka served notice of their future promise by winning the inaugural ICC Trophy in 1979, a breeding ground for their subsequent Test breakthrough. They achieved their first Test win, against New Zealand, in December 1992. Muttiah Muralitharan's off-spin has dominated their improved performances in the past five years. He is rated second only to Shane Warne (Australia) as the world's finest spin bowler. *See* **MCC.**

stance
Batsman's standing position when addressing the bowler.

stand
The accumulation of runs by a batting partnership.

standing back
Wicket-keeper's position for taking deliveries from faster bowlers.

standing up
Wicket-keeper's position close to the stumps for taking deliveries from slower bowlers.

start of play
Commencement of the day's play.

St George's Park
South African Test match ground in Port Elizabeth notorious for its batsman-friendly wicket.

sticks
Slang for the stumps.

sticky dog
Rain-affected pitch surface offering the bowlers considerable assistance. Now unusual due to use of the covers.

sticky wicket
See sticky dog.

stifled appeal
Restrained shout in the direction of the umpire by the fielding team, knowing that the batsman is unlikely to be given out.

stitching
The six lines of flax used to bind together the leather out-casing of the ball.

stock ball
Type of delivery that the bowler will try to produce the majority of the time.

stock bowler
Steady, reliable bowler employed to keep runs down and take occasional wicket when strike bowlers are resting.

stolen run
A quickly taken single.

stonewall
Defensive batting tactic employed to absorb time without losing wickets or scoring runs.

stood his ground
A batsman's decision to wait for the umpire's signal in the case of a unclear appeal.

straight bat
Stroke played with the full width of a vertical bat surface presented to the oncoming delivery.

straight drive
Attacking stroke off the front foot that dispatches the ball back past the bowler.

strategy
Preconceived match plan, often based on the condition of the pitch, the weather conditions, or the strength and weaknesses of the opposing team. *See* **game plan, match plan.**

streaky
Loose stroke in which the batsman has managed to present the minimum of bat surface to the ball.

stress fracture
Injury caused by overuse, often affecting the shins of fast bowlers.

strike bowler
Fastest bowler(s) in the attack.

striker
Batsman facing the next delivery. *See* **on strike**.

strike rate
The tempo at which an individual batsman or team score runs during an innings.

strip
The pitch.

stroke
Shot by a batsman.

strokemaker
Attacking batsman who likes to play shots.

strokeplayer
Batsman with ability to play attacking shots of textbook perfection.

stuck in the crease
Batsman rendered strokeless and shot-shy by good bowling. *See* **shot-shy**.

stud marks
Pitch surface disturbed by a bowler's boot studs.

studs
Short metal spikes driven or screwed into the soles of boots to aid foothold adhesion.

stump camera
Mini-camera inserted in stumps for worm's-eye television screening of a batsman at the wicket.

stumped
Dismissal by wicket-keeper for batsman caught out of his ground.

stumps
The six poles pitched into the playing surface, three at each end of a 22-yard strip. The top of the stumps are 28in/71.1cm above the playing surface. Also known as timbers. Can also mean the end of a day's play. *See* **castle.**

submarine ball
In Australia a bowling delivery that stays low after pitching.

substitute
Replacement player or twelfth man.

substitute fielder
Replacement fielder for injured player.

sucker punch
A soft dismissal as a result of falling victim to a game plan.

sun block
Protective cream, the main ingredient of which is zinc. Also known as war paint.

Sunday League
One-day competition played originally in England on a Sunday. Replaced by the one-day Norwich Union League of two divisions played throughout the week.

sundries
Australian equivalent for extras.

Super Fours
Women's tournament of four equally balanced sides chosen by national selectors from the top forty-eight players in an effort to narrow the gap between County and international cricket.

Super Sixes
The latter stages of the World Cup competition.

SuperSport Park
South African Test match ground, formerly known as Centurion Park, and the home of Northern Transvaal cricket. The stadium's appeal is in the vast grass embankment which represents a large proportion of the seating area.

Surrey CCC
The present club was established on 22 August 1845. The county was admitted to the official County Championship in 1890. The club colours are chocolate. The badge is the Prince of Wales's feathers. Ground: The AMP Oval, London.

Sussex CCC
Formation of he present club was on 1 March 1839. The county was admitted to the official County Championship in 1890. The club colours are dark blue, light blue and gold. The

badge is the county arms of six martlets (flightless birds). Ground: County Ground, Hove.

sweep
Attacking stroke played through the leg side with a horizontal bat.

sweeper
Fielder deployed in defensive outfield position to cut off boundary shots that have eluded the in-fielders.

sweep shot
See sweep.

sweet spot
The meat of the bat from which the ball flies with the greatest impetus when a stroke is played. *See* **meat of the bat**.

swing
Sideways movement of delivery in the air from an inswing or outswing bowler.

swing bowler
Bowler adept at making the ball move sideways in the air.

Sydney Cricket Ground
Australian Test match ground situated in the Moor Park district in the east of the city, it has a relatively limited capacity with seating for only 40,000. Since the 1970s the wicket has become a spin bowler's paradise, having been favourable for batting in its earliest incarnation.

T

tadi
Indian for a batsman's disdainful and arrogant treatment of the bowling.

take the field
The decision to field on winning the toss.

tail end
Lower order batting.

tail-ender
Batsman employed in the lower order line-up. Also referred to as rabbits because they hop around the crease, usually because they have been unsettled by quick bowling.

taken off
Bowler's withdrawal from the attack.

taking guard
Batsman's request to the umpire when calling for a guard with the bat in his blockhole before receiving the first ball of his innings. *See* **blockhole**.

talent
The natural aptitude of a player; also a young player showing ability.

talismanic player
Charismatic team member perceived to bring luck to the side.

tappa
Indian for high quality bowling.

tea interval
Break between the end of the afternoon session and the beginning of the final period of play.

team effort
A performance where everyone works for each other with every player carrying out his role with diligence and dexterity.

team spirit
Sense of camaraderie between players.

teasing delivery
Ball so cleverly delivered that it is capable of teasing the batsman into indiscretion.

teasing length
Deliveries pitched by the bowler to create doubt in a batsman's mind as to whether his initial movement should be forward or back.

teasing line
Bowler's nagging accuracy of maintaining a good direction.

telegraph
To make one's intentions obvious.

temperament
Natural character of a player and his ability to absorb pressure.

Test Championship
The ICC Test Championship was inaugurated in 2001 with England's npower Test series against Pakistan. The new competition formulates rankings for Test cricket based on results for the first time in cricket history.

Test circuit
The global stage on which the ten Test playing nations perform.

Test grounds
Arenas around the world where Test cricket is played.

testimonial match
Benefit game to raise funds for an individual, club or charitable organisation.

Test Match
International match of three or more days duration played between the ten countries that make up the Test circuit. The term Test Match was not used until the 1890s.

Test Match Special
BBC radio's commentary of cricket.

Test series
A rubber of matches, usually of three to five fixtures. *See* rubber.

Test status
Distinction afforded to countries considered to have a cricketing infrastructure of sufficient standard to play Test matches.

text book
Any performance which follows the coaching manual.

the line belongs to the umpire
Expression indicating that a batsman's bat must be over and not merely on the popping crease in order to be in his ground. *See* popping crease.

they've all gone up
Unanimous appeal by fielding side. *See* appeal.

thick edge
Ball that comes off the edge of the bat but with more contact on the blade than a 'thin' edge.

thigh pad
Leg guard worn by batsmen above the knee beneath their flannels

thin edge
A snick, the ball making minimal contact with the edge of the bat surface. *See* thick edge.

third man
Fielding position deep on the off side at a 45-degree angle to the pitch. A short third man is often used to prevent the scoring of a single.

third slip
A close catcher positioned on the right shoulder but forward of second slip to a right-handed batsman.

third umpire
Match official employed in an armchair position in the pavilion with a television screen to adjudicate line decisions that have caused difficulty for the two umpires in the middle.

throat ball
A short pitched delivery from a fast bowler that rises at the jugular rather than the top of a batsman's head.

through the gap / gate
Delivery that passes between a batsman's pad and bat.

through the line
Textbook stroke in which the batsman has hit down and through the line of the approaching ball with the full face of the bat presented during the stroke.

throw
Ball returned to the wicket by a fielder.

throw down the stumps
To hit the stumps directly from a fielding throw.

throw-in
The throw from a fielder to wicket-keeper or bowler's end, made often to attempt a run out.

throwing
Illegal bowling action with the elbow bent to generate extra pace. *See* chucking, illegal delivery.

throwing a game
To deliberately lose a match. *See* sold

throw the bat
Aggressive batting in an attempt to increase the run rate.

tickle
Stroke employed with minimum of backlift and power to work a delivery behind square on the off or leg sides. *See* backlift.

tied match
Match in which both sides have achieved the same score.

tied Test
An exceptionally rare occurrence whereby both sides post identical scores at the end of the match.

timbers
Colloquialism for the stumps. *See* stumps.

timed out
New batsman is given out if he wilfully takes more than three minutes to arrive at the crease from the pavilion.

time to be added
Play stretched beyond normal hours of play at the end of the day to compensate for time lost during the day.

time wasting
Law 42 that governs fair and unfair play stipulates that it is unfair for any member of the fielding or batting sides to waste time.

timing
Strokes played by a batsman with the minimum effort and the maximum rhythm, the ball travelling quickly off the meat of the bat.

tip and run
Unofficial version of cricket where the batsman has to run every time he hits the ball.

toe end
The bottom end of a cricket bat farthest from the handle.

tomato
Australian for a cricket ball.

ton
Hundred-run milestone achieved by a batsman. Also known as a century and a hundred.

tonk
To strike the ball with maximum force. Aggressive Essex keeper-batsman 'Tonker' Taylor, a renowned hitter, popularised the term in the 1990s.

top edge
Ball that comes off the upper edge of the bat.

top of the order
An opening batsman.

top spinner
Delivery by a spin bowler with over-spun energy imparted on the ball to make it hustle forward, rather than sideways, off the pitch.

toss, the
Coin tossing ceremony between the two captains to decide who will bat and field at the start of a match. Popularised in recent years by television whose cameras follow the skippers to the middle to record the event.

toss-up
See toss, the.

tour
An arranged series of away matches, usually abroad.

touring team
See tour side.

tour side
Squad of players chosen to fulfill series of fixtures away from home. Also known as a touring team.

track
The pitch.

trademark stroke
A batsman's speciality shot. Also known as a signature shot.

trajectory
Flight of the ball when delivered by a bowler.

trapped in the crease
Batsman rooted to the blockhole and rendered strokeless by a bowler. *See* **blockhole**.

Trent Bridge
English Test match ground at Nottingham and celebrated for its architecture which has been developed within the parameters of its 1886 pavilion.

triangular tournament
Series between three sides.

trundler
Colloquialism for a sedate, slow to medium-paced bowler.

turn
Sideways movement off the pitch of a spun ball.

turning pitch
Playing surface that encourages spin bowling by the extravagant sideways movement it offers.

turn one's arm over
Having a bowl.

turn up the heat
To increase the level of pressure.

twelfth man
Reserve player.

Twenty20 Cup
Tournament comprising a series of twenty-over matches between County sides.

twirler
Spin bowler.

two legs
A middle and leg stump guard. *See* taking guard.

Tykes
See Yorkshire County Cricket Club.

U

umbrella field
Cordon of close catchers positioned on the off and leg sides to exploit a bowler's dominance.

umpire
Match official, ususally white-coated, employed in the middle to enforce the Laws of Cricket.

umpire's bell
Audible device sounded before the start of a day's play to signal that the umpires are about to walk onto the field.

unbeaten
Undefeated innings by a batsman.

uncertainty
As in corridor of uncertainty. Ball delivered on or around the line of the off stump and pitched in an area likely to cause the batsman most uncertainty in choosing the right stroke.

uncovered pitches
Wickets left open to the weather without the protection of covers.

undefeated
Describes a batsman who remains not out at the end of an innings.

underarm
Early form of bowling in which the ball was delivered under-arm and often along the ground. It is a perfectly legitimate ball even today, providing the umpire and the striker have been informed that the bowler intends to employ this delivery. Used notoriously in 1981 by Australian player Trevor Chappell when he dispatched an underarm grubber to prevent a New Zealand batsman from scoring the six runs needed off the last ball of the match to tie a one-day international.

undercut
Backspin imparted on the ball by a bowler.

underdog
Team perceived as the most likely to lose.

underedge
Delivery striking the bottom edge of the bat.

under lights
A floodlit match.

underpitch(ed)
Delivery bowled short of a length.

understanding
An almost telepathic communication between batsmen at the wicket enabling singles to be taken without calling.

undone
When a batsman is outwitted by the bowler.

uneven bounce
Erratic climb of the ball after pitching.

unfair play
The preamble to the Laws, described as The Spirit of Cricket, says the responsibility for fair play lies with the captains to ensure that play is conducted within the spirit and traditions of the game. Law 42 governs fair and unfair play.

United Cricket Board of South Africa
The governing body of South African cricket established at the end of apartheid.

university cricket
The game played at university level. Oxford and Cambridge first met in the traditional Varsity Match at Lord's in 1927. The 2000 fixture between these old adversaries marked the end of an era. The ECB's reform of cricket dictates that Oxford become one of six new University Centres of Excellence and that the first-class Varsity Match should alternate between Fenner's and The Parks. So as not to lose the Lord's connection, an annual one-day contest between the two universities will be played at cricket's famous headquarters. Meanwhile, an annual Centres of Excellence tournament has been launched, with a final.

unorthodox
Not textbook. The opposite of compliance with accepted coaching doctrine.

unorthodox spinner
Slow bowler whose action bears no resemblance to the type of delivery bowled.

unplayable
Delivery by a bowler so good it defeats all efforts by the batsman to make contact between bat and ball.

unsight
Line of sight of a player or umpire is obscured.

uppercut
Unorthodox stroke executed by batsman to strike a rising delivery over the slip area towards the boundary. Australian Test batsman Adam Gilchrist employed the stroke to reach his century at Edgbaston in 2001. *See* **boundary**.

uppish
Injudicious shot that sends the ball into the outfield through the air rather than along the ground.

upright seam
Ball held by bowler with the stitching held parallel between two fingers of his hand.

urine treament
A method sometimes used by spinners to harden the skin on the fingers.

uses feet
Batsman's footwork employed to get to the pitch of the ball.

using the pace of the ball
Batting technique using the speed of the ball, rather than force, to beat the field.

utility player
Able to perform several functions in a team, but without a specialist role.

undone

V

V
Area between mid-off and mid-on when surveyed by the batsman taking strike.

variable bounce
An 'up and down' pitch of uneven bounce.

variable pitch
Pitch of unpredictable bounce.

variable turn
Pitch that offers a spin bowler varying degrees of turn.

variations
The bowler's ability to bowl different types of delivery to confuse the batsman.

varied attack
Mix of seam, spin and swing bowling.

Varsity Match
Annual fixture between Cambridge and Oxford universities. The traditional three-day contest was reduced to a one-day match in 2001.

vice-captain
The team captain's deputy.

Vidarbha Cricket Association Ground
Indian Test match venue in the orange city of Nagpur where the wicket has become increasingly flat lending itself to the compilation of big scores.

village
Derogatory description of a player of poor ability.

village cricket
The game as it is played on the village greens of Britain.

Village Cricket Championship
A national knockout tournament contested by village clubs for the past thirty years with a final at Lord's. Organised by The Cricketer International magazine.

virtuosity
Display of excellence performed by a player with a high degree of technical skill.

Vodafone Group
International telecommunications giant and current sponsor of the England cricket team.

volley
Batsman's hard return of the ball before it touches the ground. Also known as on the full.

vup
West Indian equivalent of the slog.

W

WACA, The

Widely used abbreviation for the Western Australian Cricket Association Test match venue in Perth.

wading in

All-out assault by the batting side on a bowling attack.

waft

Wave the bat at a delivery without making contact.

wag

Used to describe a multitude of unexpected runs from the lower order batsmen. Also a humorously outspoken spectator.

wag of the tail

Run-making flourish by the lower order batsmen to give the innings a late boost.

wagon wheel

Elaborate circular-shaped chart drawn by scorers to indicate the spread of shots round the ground made by a batsman during his innings.

wait

Instruction from one batsman to the other not to take a run.

waited for it

Batting technique which allows the ball to come on to the striker without him lunging for contact.

walk

To dismiss oneself without waiting for the umpire's decision.

walking in

The practice of fielders of moving several paces in towards the wicket as the bowler runs in to bowl so as to be able to attack the ball if it is hit in their direction.

wand

Another name for the bat.

Wankhede Stadium

Indian Test match ground in Mumbai which, due to its close proximity to the sea, assists swing bowling, particularly in the early part of the day.

warm down

Gentle exercise after a day's play to relax the muscles and avoid possible injury.

warn

Instruction from umpire to player for transgressing the Law governing fair play.

Warne, Shane
Born 1969. Celebrated Australian leg break bowler and master of his art combining a full artillery of deliveries with outstanding control.

Warner, Sir Pelham 'Plum'
See **The Cricketer International and The Forty Club**.

war paint
Slang for sun block.

Warwickshire CCC
Formation of the present club was on 8 April 1882. The county was admitted to the official County Championship in 1895. The club colours are dark blue, gold and silver. The badge is a bear and ragged staff. Ground: Edgbaston, Birmingham.

webbing
Material between the thumb and index finger on the wicket-keeper's gloves to aid catching.

well held
Appreciative exclamation in response to a cleverly taken catch.

Western Australia Cricket Ground
Located in Perth and known as 'The Waca', it is universally regarded as the fastest wicket in the world, with bowlers being assisted by the 'Fremantle Doctor', a sea breeze which drifts across the ground.

West Indies
Full members of the ICC since 1926. Their pre-war performances were largely undistinguished, but in the past thirty years they have often proved themselves to be the best side in the world. The three W's, Frank Worrell, Clyde Walcott and Everton Weekes, played the Calypso-style cricket in the 1950s that was to become the Windies trademark, and a succession of great players, namely the legendary all-rounder Garfield Sobers, Clive Lloyd and Viv Richards, have led the Caribbean kings to glorious triumph all over the world on the Test stage. They won the first two World Cups in 1975 and 1979 but lost their crown to India in the 1983 final. Record-breaking batsman Brian Lara has shouldered the mantle of responsibility almost single-handedly for much of the past decade as match-winning talent in the islands dried up and the team struggled to emulate the great feats of their predecessors. *See* **calypso cricket**.

Westpac Trust Park
Occasionally used New Zealand Test match ground close to the centre of Hamilton and renowned for its 'Village Green' setting.

whale
Machine used for mopping-up water from the outfield after rain.

wheels
Player-speak for a bowler of extreme pace.

whip
To strike the ball with the bat with strong wristwork.

whippy action
Rapid shoulder movement of bowler at the point of delivery.

white ball
Cricket ball used for one-day matches which end under power from floodlights.

White Conduit Club
Famous cricket club that played in Islington, London, that numbered one Thomas Lord among its membership. Lord, a rich wine merchant, became the founding father of Lord's cricket ground. *See* **Lord's / Marylebone Cricket Club**.

whites
Cricket flannels.

whitewash
Series or tournament dominated by one side, which results in one side winning no matches.

wicket
Stumps defended by a batsman. Also the rectangular strip of mown grass between the two sets of stumps, which measures 22 yards/20.12metres in length and 10 feet/3.05metres in width. Before the match the ground authority are responsible for the selection and preparation of the pitch. The umpires are the final judges of whether a pitch is fit for cricket to be played.

wicketcam
Television speak for the stump camera.

wicket-keeper
The fielder with the gloves and pads behind the stumps.

wicket-keeper-batsman
A wicket-keeper as adept at batting as he is with his glove work.

wicket-keepers' union
Affectionate term given to wicket-keepers to describe their often eccentric ways and pursuits common only to their trade.

wicket maiden
An over of six legitimate balls in which a wicket has fallen without a run being scored.

wicket partnership
See **partnership**.

wickets in hand
End of an innings in which some of the eleven batsmen have not batted.

wickie
Abbreviation for wicket-keeper.

wickie killer
A batsman's dangerous leg-side sweep in the direction of the wicket-keeper.

wide
Delivery bowled so high above the striking batsman or so wide of him that, in the umpire's opinion, the batsman is unable to hit the ball as governed by Law 25.

wilful obstruction
Dismissal under Law 37 for obstructing the field.

willow
The tree used for the manufacture of cricket bats.

win'ball cricket
Played with a soft ball throughout the Caribbean.

Windies
Abbreviation for the West Indies team.

windmill action
Bowler with a delivery action that resembles a working windmill.

wicket maiden

winkle
Bowler's ability to dismiss obdurate and stubbornly resistant batsman.

winning margin
The runs or wickets that separate the winners from the losers at the end of a match.

wipe
A cross-batted slog showing little regard to the coaching manual.

Wisden
The cricketers' bible. First published in 1864 by John Wisden and produced annually ever since in its familiar yellow dust jacket. The early editions were books of record without comment. In recent years the almanack has published strident opinion on all matters relating to the game. The first issue was sold for one shilling. RRP for the 2003 Wisden of 1,760 pages was £35 Now, as always, recognised as the ultimate authority on each year's cricket.

Wisden Cricket Monthly
Founded in 1979 and published every month by Wisden Cricket Magazines Ltd, a wholly owned subsidiary of John Wisden & Co Ltd in association with John Brown Publishing.

wobblers
Eccentric movement of the ball as it travels down the pitch towards the striking batsman.

women's cricket
First record of a women's cricket match was 1745 at Gosden Common near Guildford, Surrey, the home of Bramley Cricket Club. In 1934, England sent a tour party to Australia and New Zealand, and Australia toured England in 1937. The growth of the game led to the formation of the International Women's Cricket Council in Melbourne in 1958. Rachael Heyhoe-Flint gave women's cricket an enormous boost by her influence on the game in England in the 1960s and 1970s. She captained England for 12 years from 1966–1978, highlighted by England's win in the first Women's World Cup in 1973. The World Cup is now an established part of the cricket calendar with the Test circuit beginning to mirror the men's circuit in the intensity of competition and improving standards of countries.

won the toss
Success in calling 'heads or tails' at the coin tossing ceremony between the captains before the start of a match.

Worcestershire CCC
The present club was established on 11 March 1865. The county was admitted to the official County Championship in 1899. The club colours are dark green and black. The badge is 'Shield Argent a Fess between three pears sable'. Ground: New Road, Worcestershire.

workhorse
Bowler recognised for his capacity for bowling more overs than others.

working over, given a
Bowler's tactic of unsettling a batsman through short-pitched intimidatory bowling.

work the ball
Ability to manoeuvre the ball between fielders.

World Cup
One-day tournament played every four years between all the major countries and minnows qualifying from ICC Trophy finals.

world rankings
The official ratings of the ten Test playing countries, batsmen and bowlers, calculated by PriceWaterhouseCoopers, the global financial services company.

World Series Cricket
In May 1977, the story of the signing of contracts by many of Australia's leading players to the Australian television tycoon Kerry Packer shook the game. Packer employed Test players for his own series of matches. WSC lasted only a short time but it struck a blow for many impoverished Test players and persuaded the cricket authorities to improve players' remuneration. At its height, WSC had 51 of the world's top players under contract, including the England captain Tony Greig, Ian Chappell (Australia) and Clive Lloyd (West Indies). The cricket authorities called for the players to be banned but a High Court in London declared that to be 'restraint of trade' and the players won the day. *See* **Kerry Packer**.

World Test Championship
League table of the ten cricketing nations.

worn patch
Threadbare surface of pitch lacking a covering of grass.

worn pitch
Wicket surface that lacks a grass covering and has been over-used for cricket.

wrist spinner
Bowler who employs wrist rather than fingers to impart spin on the ball.

wristy
Use of wristwork in the execution of a stroke.

wrong 'un
Googly or bosie. Off-break bowled with a leg-break action by a right-hand bowler.

World Cup

X Y

XI
Roman numeral denoting the number of players in a team.

XL Club
Team with no fixed ground for the over-forties playing friendly matches against schools and clubs.

x-rated
Intimidatory fast bowling.

yahoo
Colloquialism for a batsman's rashly executed swing at the ball. *See* **blind swipe**.

yardstick
Metaphorical tool by which the comparison of standards are measured.

yellow streak
Characteristic of a cowardly player.

yips
Nervous condition affecting bowler's action resulting in his failure to release the ball correctly at the point of delivery.

yorker
Delivery speared at pace into the batsman's blockhole that often defeats the striker's efforts to jab down on the ball and keep it out of his stumps. *See* **blockhole**.

Yorkshire CCC
The present club was established on 8 January 1863. The county was admitted to the official County Championship in 1890. The club colours are dark blue, light blue and gold. The badge is a white rose. Known as the Tykes. Ground: Headingley, Leeds.

you ain't got a thing, if you ain't got that swing
Implies that a bowler unable to produce swing will be ineffectual; borrowed from the song 'It Don't Mean a Thing'.

you cannot score runs in the pavilion
Adage expressing the need of a batsman to protect his wicket.

Z

zat
Short-form appeal for 'How's that, umpire?'

zealot
Uncompromising, extreme cricket fanatic. Also known as an anorak.

zest
Used in respect of a batting or bowling performance played with relish.

Zimbabwe
Full members of the ICC since 1992. They played their first Test match that year against India at Harare Sports Club. Their captain, David Houghton, scored a maiden Test century in that match and played a crusading role in his country's development as increasingly credible Test and one-day opponents. Their first Test victory was achieved in February 1995 against Pakistan at Harare. Cricket was introduced to Rhodesia in 1890 and MCC teams toured there between the wars. Unfortunately, Rhodesia's unilateral declaration of independence (UDI) in 1966 led to their isolation by the rest of the cricket world. The mould was broken in 1983 when, as winners of the 1982 ICC Trophy, Zimbabwe competed in the World Cup in England. They beat Australia at Trent Bridge in the greatest giant-killing act in the World Cup's brief history and ran mighty West Indies close in another game.

Their subsequent elevation to Test status was inevitable from that historic breakthrough. *See* **MCC, ICC Trophy**.

Zimbabwe Cricket Union
Governing body of Zimbabwe cricket with a headquarters on the Harare Sports Ground.

zinc
The white metal derivative used in the production of sun block.

Zindabaad
Chant of Pakistan fans being Urdu for 'life, blood and soul'.

zip
Rapid movement of the ball off a hard wicket, making a low fast swishing sound as it travels through the air.

zoom
Television technology used in determining whether the ball struck the bat by providing a frame-by-frame close-up.

zooter
Delivery perfected by Australian leg-spin wizard Shane Warne that is squeezed out from between fingers, keeps low and threatens to hurry a batsman into error. An amalgamation of 'zip' and 'shoot', both suggesting rapid movement.

Fielding Positions

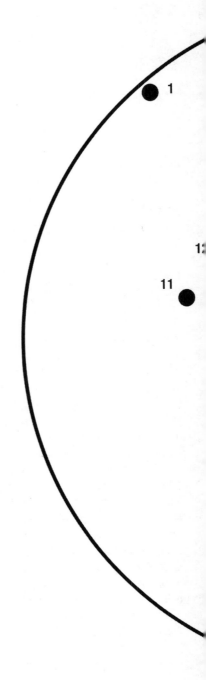

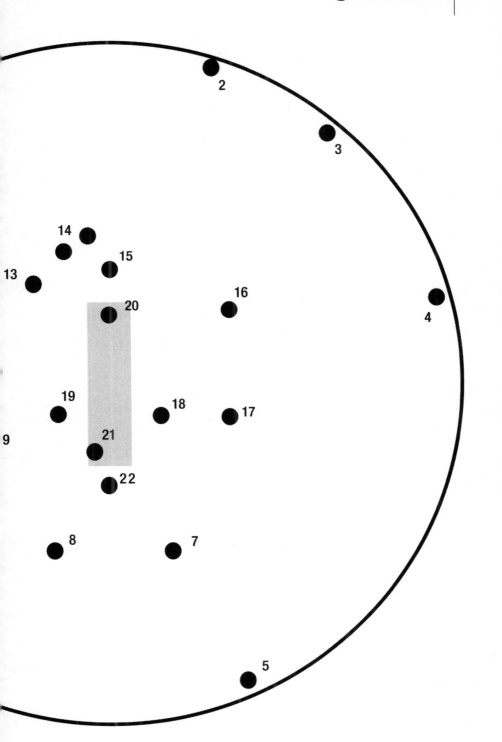

The Laws of
Cricket

(2000 Code)

Reproduced by kind permission of
the Marylebone Cricket Club

Preface

The game of Cricket has been governed by a series of Codes of Law for over 250 years. These Codes have been subject to additions and alterations recommended by the governing authorities of the time. Since its formation in 1787, the Marylebone Cricket Club (MCC) has been recognised as the sole authority for drawing up the Code and for all subsequent amendments. The Club also holds the World copyright.

The basic Laws of Cricket have stood remarkably well the test of well over 250 years of playing the game. It is thought the real reason for this is that cricketers have traditionally been prepared to play in the Spirit of the Game as well as in accordance with the Laws.

Now in 2000, MCC has revised and re-written the Laws for the new Millennium. In this Code, the major innovation is the introduction of the Spirit of Cricket as a Preamble to the Laws. Whereas in the past it was assumed that the implicit Spirit of the Game was understood and accepted by all those involved, now MCC feels it right to put into words some clear guidelines, which will help to maintain the unique character and enjoyment of the game. The other aims have been to dispense with the Notes, to incorporate all the points into the Laws and to remove, where possible, any ambiguities, so that captains, players and umpires can continue to enjoy the game at whatever level they may be playing. MCC has consulted widely with all the Full Member Countries of the International Cricket Council, the Governing Body of the game. There has been close consultation with the Association of Cricket Umpires and Scorers. The Club has also brought in umpires and players from all round the world.

Significant dates in the history of the Laws are as follows:

1700 Cricket was recognised as early as this date.

1744 The earliest known Code was drawn up by certain 'Noblemen and Gentlemen' who used the Artillery Ground in London.

1755   The Laws were revised by 'Several Cricket Clubs, particularly the Star and Garter in Pall Mall'.

1774   A further revision was produced by 'a Committee of Noblemen and Gentlemen of Kent, Hampshire, Surrey, Sussex, Middlesex and London at the Star and Garter'.

1786   A further revision was undertaken by a similar body of Noblemen and Gentlemen of Kent, Hampshire, Surrey, Sussex, Middlesex and London.

1788   The first MCC Code of Laws was adopted on 30th May.

1835   A new Code of Laws was approved by the MCC Committee on 19th May.

1884   After consultation with cricket clubs worldwide, important alterations were incorporated in a new version approved at an MCC Special General Meeting on 21st April.

1947   A new Code of Laws was approved at an MCC Special General Meeting on 7th May. The main changes were aimed at achieving clarification and better arrangement of the Laws and their interpretations. This did not, however, exclude certain definite alterations which were designed to provide greater latitude in the conduct of the game as required by the widely differing conditions in which Cricket was played.

1979   After five editions of the 1947 Code, a further revision was begun in 1974 with the aim being to remove certain anomalies, consolidate various amendments and notes, and to achieve greater clarity and simplicity. The new Code of Laws was approved at an MCC Special General Meeting on 21st November.

1992   A second edition of the 1980 Code was produced, incorporating all the amendments which were approved during the intervening twelve years.

Many queries on the Laws, which apply equally to women's cricket as to men's, are sent to MCC for decision every year. MCC, as the accepted Guardian of the Laws, which can only be changed by the vote of two-thirds of the Members at a Special General Meeting of the Club, has always been prepared to answer the queries and to give interpretations on certain conditions, which will be readily understood.

(a) In the case of league or competition cricket, the enquiry must come from the committee responsible for organising the league or competition. In other cases, enquiries should be initiated by a representative officer of a club, or of an umpires' association on behalf of his or her committee, or by a master or mistress in charge of school cricket.

(b) The incident on which a ruling is required must not be merely invented for disputation but must have actually occurred in play.

(c) The enquiry must not be connected in any way with a bet or wager.

R. D. V. Knight, Secretary MCC
Lord's Cricket Ground, London NW8 8QN
16 February 2000

Contents

The Laws of Cricket

The Preamble – The Spirit of Cricket

Cricket is a game that owes much of its unique appeal to the fact that it should be played not only within its Laws but also within the Spirit of the Game. Any action which is seen to abuse this spirit causes injury to the game itself. The major responsibility for ensuring the spirit of fair play rests with the captains.

1.   There are two Laws which place the responsibility for the team's conduct firmly on the captain.

Responsibility of captains
The captains are responsible at all times for ensuring that play is conducted within the Spirit of the Game as well as within the Laws.

Player's conduct
In the event of a player failing to comply with instructions by an umpire, or criticising by word or action the decisions of an umpire, or showing dissent, or generally behaving in a manner which might bring the game into disrepute, the umpire concerned shall in the first place report the matter to the other umpire and to the player's captain, and instruct the latter to take action.

2.   *Fair and unfair play*
According to the Laws the umpires are the sole judges of fair and unfair play. The umpires may intervene at any time and it is the responsibility of the captain to take action where required.

3.   *The umpires are authorised to intervene in cases of:*
   - Time wasting
   - Damaging the pitch
   - Dangerous or unfair bowling
   - Tampering with the ball
   - Any other action that they consider to be unfair

4.   *The Spirit of the Game involves RESPECT for:*
   - Your opponents
   - Your own captain and team
   - The role of the umpires
   - The game's traditional values

5.   *It is against the Spirit of the Game:*
   - To dispute an umpire's decision by word, action or gesture
   - To direct abusive language towards an opponent or umpire
   - To indulge in cheating or any sharp practice, for instance:
     (a) to appeal knowing that the batsman is not out
     (b) to advance towards an umpire in an aggressive manner when appealing
     (c) to seek to distract an opponent either verbally or by harassment with persistent clapping or unnecessary noise under the guise of enthusiasm and motivation of one's own side.

6.   *Violence*
   There is no place for any act of violence on the field of play.

7.   *Players*
   Captains and umpires together set the tone for the conduct of a cricket match. Every player is expected to make an important contribution to this.

The players, umpires and scorers in a game of cricket may be of either gender and the Laws apply equally to both. The use, throughout the text, of pronouns indicating the male gender is purely for brevity. Except where specifically stated otherwise, every provision of the Laws is to be read as applying to women and girls equally as to men and boys.

Law 1 – The Players

1. **Number of players**

   A match is played between two sides, each of eleven players, one of whom shall be captain.

   By agreement a match may be played between sides of more or less than eleven players, but not more than eleven players may field at any time.

2. **Nomination of players**

   Each captain shall nominate his players in writing to one of the umpires before the toss. No player may be changed after the nomination without the consent of the opposing captain.

3. **Captain**

   If at any time the captain is not available, a deputy shall act for him.
   (a) If a captain is not available during the period in which the toss is to take place, then the deputy must be responsible for the nomination of the players, if this has not already been done, and for the toss. See 2 above and Law 12.4 (The toss).
   (b) At any time after the toss, the deputy must be one of the nominated players.

4. **Responsibility of captains**

   The captains are responsible at all times for ensuring that play is conducted within the spirit and traditions of the game as well as within the Laws. See The Preamble – The Spirit of Cricket and Law 42.1 (Fair and unfair play - responsibility of captains).

Law 2 – Substitutes and Runners;
Batsman or Fielder Leaving the Field;
Batsman Retiring;
Batsman Commencing Innings

1. *Substitutes and runners*
   (a) If the umpires are satisfied that a player has been injured or become ill after the nomination of the players, they shall allow that player to have
      (i) a substitute acting instead of him in the field.
      (ii) a runner when batting.
      Any injury or illness that occurs at any time after the nomination of the players until the conclusion of the match shall be allowable, irrespective of whether play is in progress or not.
   (b) The umpires shall have discretion, for other wholly acceptable reasons, to allow a substitute for a fielder, or a runner for a batsman, at the start of the match or at any subsequent time.
   (c) A player wishing to change his shirt, boots, etc. must leave the field to do so. No substitute shall be allowed for him.

2. *Objection to substitutes*
   The opposing captain shall have no right of objection to any player acting as a substitute on the field, nor as to where the substitute shall field. However, no substitute shall act as wicket-keeper. See 3 below.

3. *Restrictions on the role of substitutes*
   A substitute shall not be allowed to bat or bowl nor to act as wicket-keeper or as captain on the field of play.

4. *A player for whom a substitute has acted*
   A player is allowed to bat, bowl or field even though a substitute has previously acted for him.

5. **Fielder absent or leaving the field**

    If a fielder fails to take the field with his side at the start of the match or at any later time, or leaves the field during a session of play,

    (a) the umpire shall be informed of the reason for his absence.

    (b) he shall not thereafter come on to the field during a session of play without the consent of the umpire. See 6 below. The umpire shall give such consent as soon as is practicable.

    (c) if he is absent for 15 minutes or longer, he shall not be permitted to bowl thereafter, subject to (i), (ii) or (iii) below, until he has been on the field for at least that length of playing time for which he was absent.

    (i) Absence or penalty for time absent shall not be carried over into a new day's play.

    (ii) If, in the case of a follow-on or forfeiture, a side fields for two consecutive innings, this restriction shall, subject to (i) above, continue as necessary into the second innings but shall not otherwise be carried over into a new innings.

    (iii) The time lost for an unscheduled break in play shall be counted as time on the field for any fielder who comes on to the field at the resumption of play. See Law 15.1 (An interval).

6. **Player returning without permission**

    If a player comes on to the field of play in contravention of 5(b) above and comes into contact with the ball while it is in play

    (i) the ball shall immediately become dead and the umpire shall award 5 penalty runs to the batting side. See Law 42.17 (Penalty runs).

    (ii) the umpire shall inform the other umpire, the captain of the fielding side, the batsmen and, as soon as practicable, the captain of the batting side of the reason for this action.

    (iii) the umpires together shall report the occurrence as soon as possible to the Executive of the fielding side and any Governing Body responsible for the match, who shall take such action as is considered appropriate against the captain and player concerned.

7. **_Runner_**

   The player acting as a runner for a batsman shall be a member of the batting side and shall, if possible, have already batted in that innings. The runner shall wear external protective equipment equivalent to that worn by the batsman for whom he runs and shall carry a bat.

8. **_Transgression of the Laws by a batsman who has a runner_**

   (a) A batsman's runner is subject to the Laws. He will be regarded as a batsman except where there are specific provisions for his role as a runner. See 7 above and Law 29.2 (Which is a batsman's ground).

   (b) A batsman with a runner will suffer the penalty for any infringement of the Laws by his runner as though he had been himself responsible for the infringement. In particular he will be out if his runner is out under any of Laws 33 (Handled the ball), 37 (Obstructing the field) or 38 (Run out).

   (c) When a batsman with a runner is striker he remains himself subject to the Laws and will be liable to the penalties that any infringement of them demands.

   Additionally, if he is out of his ground when the wicket is put down at the wicket-keeper's end, he will be out in the circumstances of Law 38 (Run out) or Law 39 (Stumped) irrespective of the position of the non-striker or of the runner. If he is thus dismissed, runs completed by the runner and the other batsman before the dismissal shall not be scored. However, the penalty for a No ball or a Wide shall stand, together with any penalties to either side that may be awarded when the ball is dead. See Law 42.17 (Penalty runs).

   (d) When a batsman with a runner is not the striker

   (i) he remains subject to Laws 33 (Handled the ball) and 37 (Obstructing the field) but is otherwise out of the game.

   (ii) he shall stand where directed by the striker's end umpire so as not to interfere with play.

   (iii) he will be liable, notwithstanding (i) above, to the penalty demanded by the Laws should he commit any act of unfair play.

9. Batsman leaving the field or retiring

A batsman may retire at any time during his innings. The umpires, before allowing play to proceed, shall be informed of the reason for a batsman retiring.

(a) If a batsman retires because of illness, injury or any other unavoidable cause, he is entitled to resume his innings subject to (c) below. If for any reason he does not do so, his innings is to be recorded as 'Retired – not out'.

(b) If a batsman retires for any reason other than as in (a) above, he may only resume his innings with the consent of the opposing captain. If for any reason he does not resume his innings it is to be recorded as 'Retired – out'.

(c) If after retiring a batsman resumes his innings, it shall be only at the fall of a wicket or the retirement of another batsman.

10. Commencement of a batsman's innings

Except at the start of a side's innings, a batsman shall be considered to have commenced his innings when he first steps on to the field of play, provided Time has not been called. The innings of the opening batsmen, and that of any new batsman at the resumption of play after a call of Time, shall commence at the call of Play.

Law 3 – The Umpires

1. Appointment and attendance

Before the match, two umpires shall be appointed, one for each end, to control the game as required by the Laws, with absolute impartiality. The umpires shall be present on the ground and report to the Executive of the ground at least 45 minutes before the scheduled start of each day's play.

2. Change of umpire

An umpire shall not be changed during the match, other than in exceptional circumstances, unless he is injured or ill. If there has to be a change of umpire, the replacement shall act only as the striker's end umpire unless the captains agree that he should take full responsibility as an umpire.

3. **Agreement with captains**

Before the toss the umpires shall

(a) ascertain the hours of play and agree with the captains

(i) the balls to be used during the match. See Law 5 (The ball).

(ii) times and durations of intervals for meals and times for drinks intervals. See Law 15 (Intervals).

(iii) the boundary of the field of play and allowances for boundaries. See Law 19 (Boundaries).

(iv) any special conditions of play affecting the conduct of the match.

(b) inform the scorers of the agreements in (ii), (iii) and (iv) above.

4. **To inform captains and scorers**

Before the toss the umpires shall agree between themselves and inform both captains and both scorers

(i) which clock or watch and back-up time piece is to be used during the match.

(ii) whether or not any obstacle within the field of play is to be regarded as a boundary. See Law 19 (Boundaries).

5. **The wickets, creases and boundaries**

Before the toss and during the match, the umpires shall satisfy themselves that

(i) the wickets are properly pitched. See Law 8 (The wickets).

(ii) the creases are correctly marked. See Law 9 (The bowling, popping and return creases).

(iii) the boundary of the field of play complies with the requirements of Law 19.2 (Defining the boundary – boundary marking).

6. **Conduct of the game, implements and equipment**

Before the toss and during the match, the umpires shall satisfy themselves that

(a) the conduct of the game is strictly in accordance with the Laws.

(b) the implements of the game conform to the requirements of Laws 5 (The ball) and 6 (The bat), together with either Laws 8.2 (Size of stumps) and 8.3 (The bails) or, if appropriate, Law 8.4 (Junior cricket).

(c) (i) no player uses equipment other than that permitted. See Appendix D.

(ii) the wicket-keeper's gloves comply with the requirements of Law 40.2 (Gloves).

7. **Fair and unfair play**

The umpires shall be the sole judges of fair and unfair play.

8. **Fitness of ground, weather and light**

The umpires shall be the final judges of the fitness of the ground, weather and light for play. See 9 below and Law 7.2 (Fitness of the pitch for play).

9. **Suspension of play for adverse conditions of ground, weather or light**

(a) (i) All references to ground include the pitch. See Law 7.1 (Area of pitch).

(ii) For the purpose of this Law and Law 15.9(b)(ii) (Intervals for drinks) only, the batsmen at the wicket may deputise for their captain at any appropriate time.

(b) If at any time the umpires together agree that the condition of the ground, weather or light is not suitable for play, they shall inform the captains and, unless

(i) in unsuitable ground or weather conditions both captains agree to continue, or to commence, or to restart play, or

(ii) in unsuitable light the batting side wish to continue, or to commence, or to restart play, they shall suspend play, or not allow play to commence or to restart.

(c) (i) After agreeing to play in unsuitable ground or weather conditions, either captain may appeal against the conditions to the umpires before the next call of Time. The umpires shall uphold the appeal only if, in their opinion, the factors taken into account when making their previous decision are the same or the conditions have further deteriorated.

(ii) After deciding to play in unsuitable light, the captain of the batting side may appeal against the light to the umpires before the next call of Time. The umpires shall uphold the appeal only if, in their opinion, the factors taken into account when making their previous decision are the same or the condition of the light has further deteriorated.

(d) If at any time the umpires together agree that the conditions of ground, weather or light are so bad that there is obvious and foreseeable risk to the safety of any player or umpire, so that it would be unreasonable or dangerous for play to take place, then notwithstanding the provisions of (b)(i) and (b)(ii) above, they shall immediately suspend play, or not allow play to commence or to restart. The decision as to whether conditions are so bad as to warrant such action is one for the umpires alone to make.

The fact that the grass and the ball are wet and slippery does not warrant the ground conditions being regarded as unreasonable or dangerous. If the umpires consider the ground is so wet or slippery as to deprive the bowler of a reasonable foothold, the fielders of the power of free movement, or the batsmen of the ability to play their strokes or to run between the wickets, then these conditions shall be regarded as so bad that it would be unreasonable for play to take place.

(e) When there is a suspension of play it is the responsibility of the umpires to monitor the conditions. They shall make inspections as often as appropriate, unaccompanied by any of the players or officials. Immediately the umpires together agree that conditions are suitable for play they shall call upon the players to resume the game.

(f) If play is in progress up to the start of an agreed interval then it will resume after the interval unless the umpires together agree that conditions are or have become unsuitable or dangerous. If they do so agree, then they shall implement the procedure in (b) or (d) above, as appropriate, whether or not there had been any decision by the captains to continue, or any appeal against the conditions by either captain, prior to the commencement of the interval.

10.   *Exceptional circumstances*

The umpires shall have the discretion to implement the procedures of 9 above for reasons other than ground, weather or light if they consider that exceptional circumstances warrant it.

11.   *Position of umpires*

The umpires shall stand where they can best see any act upon which their decision may be required.

Subject to this over-riding consideration the umpire at the bowler's end shall stand where he does not interfere with either the bowler's run up or the striker's view.

The umpire at the striker's end may elect to stand on the off side instead of the on side of the pitch, provided he informs the captain of the fielding side, the striker and the other umpire of his intention to do so.

12.   *Umpires changing ends*

The umpires shall change ends after each side has had one completed innings. See Law 14.2 (Forfeiture of an innings).

13.   *Consultation between umpires*

All disputes shall be determined by the umpires. The umpires shall consult with each other whenever necessary. See also Law 27.6 (Consultation by umpires).

14.   *Signals*

(a) The following code of signals shall be used by umpires.

    (i)   Signals made while the ball is in play

         Dead ball   — by crossing and re-crossing the wrists below the waist.

No ball	— by extending one arm horizontally.
Out	— by raising an index finger above the head. (If not out the umpire shall call Not out.)
Wide	— by extending both arms horizontally.

(ii) When the ball is dead, the signals above, with the exception of the signal for Out, shall be repeated to the scorers. The signals listed below shall be made to the scorers only when the ball is dead.

Boundary 4	— by waving an arm from side to side finishing with the arm across the chest.
Boundary 6	— by raising both arms above the head.
Bye	— by raising an open hand above the head.
Commencement of last hour	— by pointing to a raised wrist with the other hand.
Five penalty runs awarded the batting side	— by repeated tapping of one to shoulder with the opposite hand.
Five penalty runs awarded to the fielding side	— by placing one hand on the opposite shoulder.
Leg bye	— by touching a raised knee with the hand.
New ball	— by holding the ball above the head.
Revoke last signal	— by touching both shoulders, each with the opposite hand.
Short run	— by bending one arm upwards

and touching the nearer shoulder with the tips of the fingers.

(b) The umpires shall wait until each signal to the scorers has been separately acknowledged by a scorer before allowing play to proceed.

15. *Correctness of scores*

Consultation between umpires and scorers on doubtful points is essential. The umpires shall satisfy themselves as to the correctness of the number of runs scored, the wickets that have fallen and, where appropriate, the number of overs bowled. They shall agree these with the scorers at least at every interval, other than a drinks interval, and at the conclusion of the match. See Laws 4.2 (Correctness of scores), 21.8 (Correctness of result) and 21.10 (Result not to be changed).

Law 4 – The Scorers

1. *Appointment of scorers*

Two scorers shall be appointed to record all runs scored, all wickets taken and, where appropriate, number of overs bowled.

2. *Correctness of scores*

The scorers shall frequently check to ensure that their records agree. They shall agree with the umpires, at least at every interval, other than a drinks interval, and at the conclusion of the match, the runs scored, the wickets that have fallen and, where appropriate, the number of overs bowled. See Law 3.15 (Correctness of scores).

3. *Acknowledging signals*

The scorers shall accept all instructions and signals given to them by the umpires. They shall immediately acknowledge each separate signal.

Law 5 – The Ball

1. ### Weight and size

   The ball, when new, shall weigh not less than 5½ ounces/155.9g, nor more than 5¾ ounces/163g, and shall measure not less than 8 13/16 in/22.4cm, nor more than 9 in/22.9cm in circumference.

2. ### Approval and control of balls

   (a) All balls to be used in the match, having been approved by the umpires and captains, shall be in the possession of the umpires before the toss and shall remain under their control throughout the match.

   (b) The umpire shall take possession of the ball in use at the fall of each wicket, at the start of any interval and at any interruption of play.

3. ### New ball

   Unless an agreement to the contrary has been made before the match, either captain may demand a new ball at the start of each innings.

4. ### New ball in match of more than one day's duration

   In a match of more than one day's duration, the captain of the fielding side may demand a new ball after the prescribed number of overs has been bowled with the old one. The Governing Body for cricket in the country concerned shall decide the number of overs applicable in that country, which shall not be less than 75 overs.

   The umpires shall indicate to the batsmen and the scorers whenever a new ball is taken into play.

5. ### Ball lost or becoming unfit for play

   If, during play, the ball cannot be found or recovered or the umpires agree that it has become unfit for play through normal use, the umpires shall replace it with a ball which has had wear comparable with that which the previous ball had received before the need for its replacement. When the ball is replaced the umpires shall inform the batsmen and the fielding captain.

6. **Specifications**

The specifications as described in 1 above shall apply to men's cricket only. The following specifications will apply to

(i) *Women's cricket*
Weight: from $4^{15}/_{16}$ ounces/140g to $5^{5}/_{16}$ ounces /151g
Circumference: from 8¼ in/21.0cm to $8^{7}/_{8}$ in/22.5cm

(ii) *Junior cricket – under 13*
Weight: from $4^{11}/_{16}$ ounces/133g to $5^{1}/_{16}$ ounces/144g
Circumference: from $8^{1}/_{16}$ in/20.5cm to $8^{11}/_{16}$ in/22.0cm

---

Law 6 – The Bat

1. **Width and length**

The bat overall shall not be more than 38 inches/96.5cm in length. The blade of the bat shall be made solely of wood and shall not exceed 4¼ inches/10.8cm at the widest part.

2. **Covering the blade**

The blade may be covered with material for protection, strengthening or repair. Such material shall not exceed $^{1}/_{16}$ inches/1.56mm in thickness, and shall not be likely to cause unacceptable damage to the ball.

3. **Hand or glove to count as part of bat**

In these Laws,

(a) reference to the bat shall imply that the bat is held by the batsman.

(b) contact between the ball and either

(i) the striker's bat itself or

(ii) the striker's hand holding the bat or

(iii) any part of a glove worn on the striker's hand holding the bat shall be regarded as the ball striking or touching the bat, or being struck by the bat.

Law 7 – The Pitch

1. ### Area of pitch
   The pitch is a rectangular area of the ground 22 yards/20.12m in length and 10ft/3.05m in width. It is bounded at either end by the bowling creases and on either side by imaginary lines, one each side of the imaginary line joining the centres of the two middle stumps, each parallel to it and 5ft/1.52m from it. See Laws 8.1 (Width and pitching) and 9.2 (The bowling crease).

2. ### Fitness of the pitch for play
   The umpires shall be the final judges of the fitness of the pitch for play. See Laws 3.8 (Fitness of ground, weather and light) and 3.9 (Suspension of play for adverse conditions of ground, weather or light).

3. ### Selection and preparation
   Before the match, the Ground Authority shall be responsible for the selection and preparation of the pitch. During the match, the umpires shall control its use and maintenance.

4. ### Changing the pitch
   The pitch shall not be changed during the match unless the umpires decide that it is unreasonable or dangerous for play to continue on it and then only with the consent of both captains.

5. ### Non-turf pitches
   In the event of a non-turf pitch being used, the artificial surface shall conform to the following measurements:

Length — a minimum of 58ft/17.68m
Width — a minimum of 6ft/1.83m
See Law 10.8 (Non-turf pitches).

Law 8 – The Wickets

1. ### Width and pitching
   Two sets of wickets shall be pitched opposite and parallel to each other at a distance of 22 yards/20.12m between the centres of the two middle stumps. Each set shall be 9 in/22.86cm wide and shall consist of three wooden stumps with two wooden bails on top. See Appendix A.

2. ### Size of stumps
   The tops of the stumps shall be 28 inches/71.1cm above the playing surface and shall be dome shaped except for the bail grooves. The portion of a stump above the playing surface shall be cylindrical, apart from the domed top, with circular section of diameter not less than 1 3/8 in/3.49cm nor more than 1½ in/3.81cm. See Appendix A.

3. ### The bails
   (a) The bails, when in position on the top of the stumps,
       (i) shall not project more than ½ in/1.27cm above them.
       (ii) shall fit between the stumps without forcing them out of the vertical.
   (b) Each bail shall conform to the following specifications. See Appendix A.

Overall length:	— 4 5/16 in/10.95cm
Length of barrel:	— 2 1/8 in/5.40cm
Longer spigot:	— 1 3/8 in/3.49cm
Shorter spigot:	— 1 3/16 in/2.06cm

4. ### Junior cricket
   In junior cricket, the same definitions of the wickets shall apply subject to

following measurements being used.

Width:	–	8 in/20.32cm
Pitched for under 13:	–	21 yards/19.20m
Pitched for under 11:	–	20 yards/18.29m
Pitched for under 9:	–	18 yards/16.46m
Height above playing surface:	–	27 in/68.58cm

Each stump

Diameter:	– not less than 1¼ in/3.18cm nor more than 1³/₈ in/3.49cm

Each bail

Overall:	–	3¹³/₁₆ in/9.68cm
Barrel:	–	1¹³/₁₆ in/4.60cm
Longer Spigot:	–	1¼ in/3.18cm
Shorter Spigot:	–	³/₄ in/1.91cm

5.   **Dispensing with bails**

The umpires may agree to dispense with the use of bails, if necessary. If they so agree then no bails shall be used at either end. The use of bails shall be resumed as soon as conditions permit. See Law 28.4 (Dispensing with bails).

Law 9 – The Bowling, Popping and Return Creases

1.   **The creases**

A bowling crease, a popping crease and two return creases shall be marked in white, as set out in 2, 3 and 4 below, at each end of the pitch. See Appendix B.

2.   **The bowling crease**

The bowling crease, which is the back edge of the crease marking, shall be the line through the centres of the three stumps at that end. It shall be 8ft 8 in/2.64m in length, with the stumps in the centre.

3. ***The popping crease***

The popping crease, which is the back edge of the crease marking, shall be in front of and parallel to the bowling crease and shall be 4ft/1.22m from it. The popping crease shall be marked to a minimum of 6ft/1.83m on either side of the imaginary line joining the centres of the middle stumps and shall be considered to be unlimited in length.

4. ***The return creases***

The return creases, which are the inside edges of the crease markings, shall be at right angles to the popping crease at a distance of 4ft 4 in/1.32m either side of the imaginary line joining the centres of the two middle stumps. Each return crease shall be marked from the popping crease to a minimum of 8ft/2.44m behind it and shall be considered to be unlimited in length.

Law 10 – Preparation and Maintenance of the Playing Area

1. ***Rolling***

The pitch shall not be rolled during the match except as permitted in (a) and (b) below.

(a) *Frequency and duration of rolling*

During the match the pitch may be rolled at the request of the captain of the batting side, for a period of not more than 7 minutes, before the start of each innings, other than the first innings of the match, and before the start of each subsequent day's play. See (d) below.

(b) *Rolling after a delayed start*

In addition to the rolling permitted above, if, after the toss and before the first innings of the match, the start is delayed, the captain of the batting side may request to have the pitch rolled for not more than 7 minutes. However, if the umpires together agree that the delay has had no significant effect on the state of the pitch, they shall refuse the request for the rolling of the pitch.

(c) *Choice of rollers*

If there is more than one roller available the captain of the batting side shall have the choice.

(d) *Timing of permitted rolling*

The rolling permitted (maximum 7 minutes) before play begins on any day shall be started not more than 30 minutes before the time scheduled or rescheduled for play to begin. The captain of the batting side may, however, delay the start of such rolling until not less than 10 minutes before the time scheduled or rescheduled for play to begin, should he so desire.

(e) *Insufficient time to complete rolling*

If a captain declares an innings closed, or forfeits an innings, or enforces the follow-on, and the other captain is prevented thereby from exercising his option of the rolling permitted (maximum 7 minutes), or if he is so prevented for any other reason, the extra time required to complete the rolling shall be taken out of the normal playing time.

2. **Sweeping**

(a) If rolling is to take place the pitch shall first be swept to avoid any possible damage by rolling in debris. This sweeping shall be done so that the 7 minutes allowed for rolling is not affected.

(b) The pitch shall be cleared of any debris at all intervals for meals, between innings and at the beginning of each day, not earlier than 30 minutes nor later than 10 minutes before the time scheduled or rescheduled for play to begin. See Law 15.1 (An interval).

(c) Notwithstanding the provisions of (a) and (b) above, the umpires shall not allow sweeping to take place where they consider it may be detrimental to the surface of the pitch.

3. **Mowing**

(a) *The pitch*

The pitch shall be mown on each day of the match on which play is expected to take place, if ground and weather conditions allow.

(b) *The outfield*

In order to ensure that conditions are as similar as possible for both sides, the outfield shall be mown on each day of the match on which play is expected to take place, if ground and weather conditions allow.

If, for reasons other than ground and weather conditions, complete mowing of the outfield is not possible, the Ground Authority shall notify the captains and umpires of the procedure to be adopted for such mowing during the match.

(c) *Responsibility for mowing*

All mowings which are carried out before the match shall be the responsibility of the Ground Authority.

All subsequent mowings shall be carried out under the supervision of the umpires.

(d) *Timing of mowing*

(i) Mowing of the pitch on any day of the match shall be completed not later than 30 minutes before the time scheduled or rescheduled for play to begin on that day.

(ii) Mowing of the outfield on any day of the match shall be completed not later than 15 minutes before the time scheduled or rescheduled for play to begin on that day.

4. *Watering*

The pitch shall not be watered during the match.

5. *Re-marking creases*

The creases shall be re-marked whenever either umpire considers it necessary.

6. *Maintenance of footholes*

The umpires shall ensure that the holes made by the bowlers and batsmen are cleaned out and dried whenever necessary to facilitate play. In matches of more than one day's duration, the umpires shall allow, if necessary, the re-turfing of footholes made by the bowler in his delivery stride, or the use of quick-setting fillings for the same purpose.

7. *Securing of footholds and maintenance of pitch*
During play, the umpires shall allow the players to secure their footholds by the use of sawdust provided that no damage to the pitch is caused and that Law 42 (Fair and unfair play) is not contravened.

8. *Non-turf pitches*
Wherever appropriate, the provisions set out in 1 to 7 above shall apply.

Law 11 – Covering the Pitch

1. *Before the match*
The use of covers before the match is the responsibility of the Ground Authority and may include full covering if required. However, the Ground Authority shall grant suitable facility to the captains to inspect the pitch before the nomination of their players and to the umpires to discharge their duties as laid down in Laws 3 (The umpires), 7 (The pitch), 8 (The wickets), 9 (The bowling, popping and return creases) and 10 (Preparation and maintenance of the playing area).

2. *During the match*
The pitch shall not be completely covered during the match unless provided otherwise by regulations or by agreement before the toss.

3. *Covering bowlers' run ups*
Whenever possible, the bowlers' run ups shall be covered in inclement weather, in order to keep them dry. Unless there is agreement for full covering under 2 above the covers so used shall not extend further than 5ft/1.52m in front of each popping crease.

4. *Removal of covers*

(a) If after the toss the pitch is covered overnight, the covers shall be removed in the morning at the earliest possible moment on each day that play is expected to take place.

(b) If covers are used during the day as protection from inclement weather, or if inclement weather delays the removal of overnight covers, they shall be removed promptly as soon as conditions allow.

Law – 12 Innings

1. *Number of innings*

(a) A match shall be one or two innings of each side according to agreement reached before the match.

(b) It may be agreed to limit any innings to a number of overs or by a period of time. If such an agreement is made then

(i) in a one innings match it shall apply to both innings.

(ii) in a two innings match it shall apply to either the first innings of each side or the second innings of each side or both innings of each side.

2. *Alternate innings*

In a two innings match each side shall take their innings alternately except in the cases provided for in Law 13 (The follow-on) or Law 14.2 (Forfeiture of an innings).

3. *Completed innings*

A side's innings is to be considered as completed if

(a) the side is all out or

(b) at the fall of a wicket, further balls remain to be bowled, but no further batsman is available to come in or

(c) the captain declares the innings closed or

(d) the captain forfeits the innings or

(e) in the case of an agreement under 1(b) above, either
  (i) the prescribed number of overs has been bowled or
  (ii) the prescribed time has expired.

4. *The toss*

The captains shall toss for the choice of innings on the field of play not earlier than 30 minutes, nor later than 15 minutes, before the scheduled or any rescheduled time for the match to start. Note, however, the provisions of Law 1.3 (Captain).

5. *Decision to be notified*

The captain of the side winning the toss shall notify the opposing captain of his decision to bat or to field, not later than 10 minutes before the scheduled or any rescheduled time for the match to start. Once notified the decision may not be altered.

Law 13 – The Follow-on

1. *Lead on first innings*

(a) In a two innings match of 5 days or more, the side which bats first and leads by at least 200 runs shall have the option of requiring the other side to follow their innings.
(b) The same option shall be available in two innings matches of shorter duration with the minimum required leads as follows:
  (i) 150 runs in a match of 3 or 4 days;
  (ii) 100 runs in a 2-day match;
  (iii) 75 runs in a 1-day match.

2. *Notification*

A captain shall notify the opposing captain and the umpires of his intention to take up this option. Law 10.1(e) (Insufficient time to complete rolling) shall apply.

3.   *First day's play lost*

If no play takes place on the first day of a match of more than one day's duration, 1 above shall apply in accordance with the number of days remaining from the actual start of the match. The day on which play first commences shall count as a whole day for this purpose, irrespective of the time at which play starts. Play will have taken place as soon as, after the call of Play, the first over has started. See Law 22.2 (Start of an over).

Law 14 – Declaration and Forfeiture

1.   *Time of declaration*

The captain of the batting side may declare an innings closed, when the ball is dead, at any time during a match.

2.   *Forfeiture of an innings*

A captain may forfeit either of his side's innings. A forfeited innings shall be considered as a completed innings.

3.   *Notification*

A captain shall notify the opposing captain and the umpires of his decision to declare or to forfeit an innings. Law 10.1(e) (Insufficient time to complete rolling) shall apply.

Law 15 – Intervals

1.   *An interval*

The following shall be classed as intervals.

(i)   The period between close of play on one day and the start of the next day's play.

(ii)   Intervals between innings.

(iii) Intervals for meals.

(iv) Intervals for drinks.

(v) Any other agreed interval.

All these intervals shall be considered as scheduled breaks for the purposes of Law 2.5 (Fielder absent or leaving the field).

2. **Agreement of intervals**

(a) Before the toss:

(i) the hours of play shall be established;

(ii) except as in (b) below, the timing and duration of intervals for meals shall be agreed;

(iii) the timing and duration of any other interval under 1(v) above shall be agreed.

(b) In a one-day match no specific time need be agreed for the tea interval. It may be agreed instead to take this interval between the innings.

(c) Intervals for drinks may not be taken during the last hour of the match, as defined in Law 16.6 (Last hour of match – number of overs). Subject to this limitation the captains and umpires shall agree the times for such intervals, if any, before the toss and on each subsequent day not later than 10 minutes before play is scheduled to start. See also Law 3.3 (Agreement with captains).

3. **Duration of intervals**

(a) An interval for lunch or for tea shall be of the duration agreed under 2(a) above, taken from the call of Time before the interval until the call of Play on resumption after the interval.

(b) An interval between innings shall be 10 minutes from the close of an innings to the call of Play for the start of the next innings, except as in 4, 6 and 7 below.

4. **No allowance for interval between innings**

In addition to the provisions of 6 and 7 below,

(a) if an innings ends when 10 minutes or less remain before the time agreed for close of play on any day, there will be no further play on that day. No change will be made to the time for the start of play on the following day on account of the 10 minutes between innings.

(b) if a captain declares an innings closed during an interruption in play of more than 10 minutes duration, no adjustment shall be made to the time for resumption of play on account of the 10 minutes between innings, which shall be considered as included in the interruption. Law 10.1(e) (Insufficient time to complete rolling) shall apply.

(c) if a captain declares an innings closed during any interval other than an interval for drinks, the interval shall be of the agreed duration and shall be considered to include the 10 minutes between innings. Law 10.1(e) (Insufficient time to complete rolling) shall apply.

Law 15

5. *Changing agreed times for intervals*

If for adverse conditions of ground, weather or light, or for any other reason, playing time is lost, the umpires and captains together may alter the time of the lunch interval or of the tea interval. See also 6, 7 and 9(c) below.

6. *Changing agreed time for lunch interval*

(a) If an innings ends when 10 minutes or less remain before the agreed time for lunch, the interval shall be taken immediately. It shall be of the agreed length and shall be considered to include the 10 minutes between innings.

(b) If, because of adverse conditions of ground, weather or light, or in exceptional circumstances, a stoppage occurs when 10 minutes or less remain before the agreed time for lunch then, notwithstanding 5 above, the interval shall be taken immediately. It shall be of the agreed length. Play shall resume at the end of this interval or as soon after as conditions permit.

(c) If the players have occasion to leave the field for any reason when more than 10 minutes remain before the agreed time for lunch then, unless the umpires and captains together agree to alter it, lunch will be taken at the agreed time.

7. *Changing agreed time for tea interval*
   (a) (i) If an innings ends when 30 minutes or less remain before the agreed time for tea, then the interval shall be taken immediately. It shall be of the agreed length and shall be considered to include the 10 minutes between innings.
   (ii) If, when 30 minutes remain before the agreed time for tea, an interval between innings is already in progress, play will resume at the end of the 10 minute interval.
   (b) (i) If, because of adverse conditions of ground, weather or light, or in exceptional circumstances, a stoppage occurs when 30 minutes or less remain before the agreed time for tea, then unless either there is an agreement to change the time for tea, as permitted in 5 above or the captains agree to forgo the tea interval, as permitted in 10 below the interval shall be taken immediately. The interval shall be of the agreed length. Play shall resume at the end of this interval or as soon after as conditions permit.
   (ii) If a stoppage is already in progress when 30 minutes remain before the time agreed for tea, 5 above will apply.

8. *Tea interval – 9 wickets down*
   If 9 wickets are down at the end of the over in progress when the agreed time for the tea interval has been reached, then play shall continue for a period not exceeding 30 minutes, unless the players have cause to leave the field of play, or the innings is concluded earlier.

9. *Intervals for drinks*
   (a) If on any day the captains agree that there shall be intervals for drinks, the option to take such intervals shall be available to either side. Each

interval shall be kept as short as possible and in any case shall not exceed 5 minutes.

(b) (i) Unless both captains agree to forgo any drinks interval, it shall be taken at the end of the over in progress when the agreed time is reached. If, however, a wicket falls within 5 minutes of the agreed time then drinks shall be taken immediately. No other variation in the timing of drinks intervals shall be permitted except as provided for in (c) below.

(ii) For the purpose of (i) above and Law 3.9(a)(ii) (Suspension of play for adverse conditions of ground, weather or light) only, the batsmen at the wicket may deputise for their captain.

(c) If an innings ends or the players have to leave the field of play for any other reason within 30 minutes of the agreed time for a drinks interval, the umpires and captains together may rearrange the timing of drinks intervals in that session.

10. *Agreement to forgo intervals*

At any time during the match, the captains may agree to forgo the tea interval or any of the drinks intervals. The umpires shall be informed of the decision.

11. *Scorers to be informed*

The umpires shall ensure that the scorers are informed of all agreements about hours of play and intervals, and of any changes made thereto as permitted under this Law.

Law 16 – Start of Play; Cessation of Play

1. *Call of Play*

The umpire at the bowler's end shall call Play at the start of the match and on the resumption of play after any interval or interruption.

2. **Call of Time**

The umpire at the bowler's end shall call Time on the cessation of play before any interval or interruption of play and at the conclusion of the match. See Law 27(Appeals).

3. **Removal of bails**

After the call of Time, the bails shall be removed from both wickets.

4. **Starting a new over**

Another over shall always be started at any time during the match, unless an interval is to be taken in the circumstances set out in 5 below, if the umpire, after walking at his normal pace, has arrived at his position behind the stumps at the bowler's end before the time agreed for the next interval, or for the close of play, has been reached.

5. **Completion of an over**

Other than at the end of the match,

(a) if the agreed time for an interval is reached during an over, the over shall be completed before the interval is taken except as provided for in (b) below.

(b) when less than 2 minutes remain before the time agreed for the next interval, the interval will be taken immediately if either

   (i) a batsman is out or retires or

   (ii) the players have occasion to leave the field whether this occurs during an over or at the end of an over. Except at the end of an innings, if an over is thus interrupted it shall be completed on resumption of play.

6. **Last hour of match – number of overs**

When one hour of playing time of the match remains, according to the agreed hours of play, the over in progress shall be completed. The next over shall be the first of a minimum of 20 overs which must be bowled, provided that a result is not reached earlier and provided that there is no interval or interruption in play. The umpire at the bowler's end shall indicate the commencement of this 20 overs to the players and the scorers. The period of play thereafter shall be referred to as the last hour, whatever its actual duration.

7. ***Last hour of match – interruptions of play***

If there is an interruption in play during the last hour of the match, the minimum number of overs to be bowled shall be reduced from 20 as follows.

(a) The time lost for an interruption is counted from the call of Time until the time for resumption of play as decided by the umpires.

(b) One over shall be deducted for every complete 3 minutes of time lost.

(c) In the case of more than one such interruption, the minutes lost shall not be aggregated; the calculation shall be made for each interruption separately.

(d) If, when one hour of playing time remains, an interruption is already in progress,

    (i) only the time lost after this moment shall be counted in the calculation;

    (ii) the over in progress at the start of the interruption shall be completed on resumption of play and shall not count as one of the minimum number of overs to be bowled.

(e) If, after the start of the last hour, an interruption occurs during an over, the over shall be completed on resumption of play. The two part-overs shall between them count as one over of the minimum number to be bowled.

8. ***Last hour of match – intervals between innings***

If an innings ends so that a new innings is to be started during the last hour of the match, the interval starts with the end of the innings and is to end 10 minutes later.

(a) If this interval is already in progress at the start of the last hour, then to determine the number of overs to be bowled in the new innings, calculations are to be made as set out in 7 above.

(b) If the innings ends after the last hour has started, two calculations are to be made, as set out in (c) and (d) below. The greater of the numbers yielded by these two calculations is to be the minimum number of overs to be bowled in the new innings.

(c) *Calculation based on overs remaining.*
   (i) At the conclusion of the innings, the number of overs that remain to be bowled, of the minimum in the last hour, to be noted.
   (ii) If this is not a whole number it is to be rounded up to the next whole number.
   (iii) Three overs to be deducted from the result for the interval.

(d) *Calculation based on time remaining.*
   (i) At the conclusion of the innings, the time remaining until the agreed time for close of play to be noted.
   (ii) Ten minutes to be deducted from this time, for the interval, to determine the playing time remaining.
   (iii) A calculation to be made of one over for every complete 3 minutes of the playing time remaining, plus one more over for any further part of 3 minutes remaining.

9. **Conclusion of match**

The match is concluded

(a) as soon as a result, as defined in sections 1,2,3 or 4 of Law 21 (The result), is reached.

(b) as soon as both
   (i) the minimum number of overs for the last hour are completed and
   (ii) the agreed time for close of play is reached unless a result has been reached earlier.

(c) if, without the match being concluded either as in (a) or in (b) above, the players leave the field, either for adverse conditions of ground, weather or light, or in exceptional circumstances, and no further play is possible thereafter.

10. *Completion of last over of match*

The over in progress at the close of play on the final day shall be completed unless either

(i) a result has been reached or

(ii) the players have occasion to leave the field. In this case there shall be no resumption of play, except in the circumstances of Law 21.9 (Mistakes in scoring), and the match shall be at an end.

11. *Bowler unable to complete an over during last hour of match*

If, for any reason, a bowler is unable to complete an over during the last hour, Law 22.8 (Bowler incapacitated or suspended during an over) shall apply.

Law 17 – Practice on the Field

1. *Practice on the field*

(a) There shall be no bowling or batting practice on the pitch, or on the area parallel and immediately adjacent to the pitch, at any time on any day of the match.

(b) There shall be no bowling or batting practice on any other part of the square on any day of the match, except before the start of play or after the close of play on that day. Practice before the start of play

(i) must not continue later than 30 minutes before the scheduled time or any rescheduled time for play to start on that day.

(ii) shall not be allowed if the umpires consider that, in the prevailing conditions of ground and weather, it will be detrimental to the surface of the square.

(c) There shall be no practice on the field of play between the call of Play and the call of Time, if the umpire considers that it could result in a waste of time. See Law 42.9 (Time wasting by the fielding side).

(d) If a player contravenes (a) or (b) above he shall not be allowed to bowl until at least 5 complete overs have been bowled by his side after the contravention. If an over is in progress at the contravention he shall not be allowed to complete that over nor shall the remaining part-over count towards the 5 overs above.

2. **Trial run up**

No bowler shall have a trial run up between the call of Play and the call of Time unless the umpire is satisfied that it will not cause any waste of time.

Law 18 – Scoring Runs

1. **A run**

The score shall be reckoned by runs. A run is scored

(a) so often as the batsmen, at any time while the ball is in play, have crossed and made good their ground from end to end.

(b) when a boundary is scored. See Law 19 (Boundaries).

(c) when penalty runs are awarded. See 6 below.

(d) when Lost ball is called. See Law 20 (Lost ball).

2. **Runs disallowed**

Notwithstanding 1 above, or any other provisions elsewhere in the Laws, the scoring of runs or awarding of penalties will be subject to any disallowance of runs provided for within the Laws that may be applicable.

3. **Short runs**

(a) A run is short if a batsman fails to make good his ground on turning for a further run.

(b) Although a short run shortens the succeeding one, the latter if completed shall not be regarded as short. A striker taking stance in front of his popping crease may run from that point also without penalty.

4. **Unintentional short runs**

Except in the circumstances of 5 below,

(a) if either batsman runs a short run, unless a boundary is scored the umpire concerned shall call and signal Short run as soon as the ball becomes dead and that run shall not be scored.

(b) if, after either or both batsmen run short, a boundary is scored, the umpire concerned shall disregard the short running and shall not call or signal Short run.

(c) if both batsmen run short in one and the same run, this shall be regarded as only one short run.

(d) if more than one run is short then, subject to (b) and (c) above, all runs so called shall not be scored.

If there has been more than one short run the umpire shall inform the scorers as to the number of runs scored.

5.   *Deliberate short runs*

(a) Notwithstanding 4 above, if either umpire considers that either or both batsmen deliberately run short at his end, the following procedure shall be adopted.

   (i)   The umpire concerned shall, when the ball is dead, warn the batsman or batsmen that the practice is unfair, indicate that this is a first and final warning and inform the other umpire of what has occurred.

   (ii) The batsmen shall return to their original ends.

   (iii) Whether a batsman is dismissed or not, the umpire at the bowler's end shall disallow all runs to the batting side from that delivery other than the penalty for a No ball or Wide, or penalties under Laws 42.5 (Deliberate distraction or obstruction of batsman) and 42.13 (Fielders damaging the pitch), if applicable.

   (iv) The umpire at the bowler's end shall inform the scorers as to the number of runs scored.

(b) If there is any further instance of deliberate short running by either of the same batsmen in that innings, when the ball is dead the umpire concerned shall inform the other umpire of what has occurred and the procedure set out in (a)(ii) and (iii) above shall be repeated. Additionally, the umpire at the bowler's end shall

(i) award 5 penalty runs to the fielding side. See Law 42.17 (Penalty runs).

(ii) inform the scorers as to the number of runs scored.

(iii) inform the batsmen, the captain of the fielding side and, as soon as practicable, the captain of the batting side of the reason for this action.

(iv) report the occurrence, with the other umpire, to the Executive of the batting side and any Governing Body responsible for the match, who shall take such action as is considered appropriate against the captain and player or players concerned.

6.   *Runs scored for penalties*
Runs shall be scored for penalties under 5 above and Laws 2.6 (Player returning without permission), 24 (No ball), 25 (Wide ball), 41.2 (Fielding the ball), 41.3 (Protective helmets belonging to the fielding side) and 42 (Fair and unfair play).

7.   *Runs scored for boundaries*
Runs shall be scored for boundary allowances under Law 19 (Boundaries).

8.   *Runs scored for Lost ball*
Runs shall be scored when Lost ball is called under Law 20 (Lost ball).

9.   *Batsman dismissed*
When either batsman is dismissed
(a) any penalties to either side that may be applicable shall stand but no other runs shall be scored, except as stated in 10 below. Note, however, Law 42.17(b) (Penalty runs).
(b) 12(a) below will apply if the method of dismissal is Caught, Handled the ball or Obstructing the field. 12(a) will also apply if a batsman is Run out, except in the circumstances of Law 2.8 (Transgression of the Laws by a batsman who has a runner) where 12(b) below will apply.

(c) the not out batsman shall return to his original end except as stated in (b) above.

10. *Runs scored when a batsman is dismissed*

In addition to any penalties to either side that may be applicable, if a batsman is

(a) dismissed Handled the ball, the batting side shall score the runs completed before the offence.

(b) dismissed Obstructing the field, the batting side shall score the runs completed before the offence. If, however, the obstruction prevents a catch from being made, no runs other than penalties shall be scored.

(c) dismissed Run out, the batting side shall score the runs completed before the dismissal. If, however, a striker with a runner is himself dismissed Run out, no runs other than penalties shall be scored. See Law 2.8 (Transgression of the Laws by a batsman who has a runner).

11. *Runs scored when ball becomes dead*

(a) When the ball becomes dead on the fall of a wicket, runs shall be scored as laid down in 9 and 10 above.

(b) When the ball becomes dead for any reason other than the fall of a wicket, or is called dead by an umpire, unless there is specific provision otherwise in the Laws, the batting side shall be credited with

  (i) all runs completed by the batsmen before the incident or call and

  (ii) the run in progress if the batsmen have crossed at the instant of the incident or call. Note specifically, however, the provisions of Laws 34.4(c) (Runs permitted from ball lawfully struck more than once) and 42.5(b)(iii) (Deliberate distraction or obstruction of batsman) and

  (iii) any penalties that are applicable.

12. *Batsman returning to wicket he has left*

(a) If, while the ball is in play, the batsmen have crossed in running, neither shall return to the wicket he has left, except as in (b) below.

(b) The batsmen shall return to the wickets they originally left in the cases of, and only in the cases of

(i) a boundary;

(ii) disallowance of runs for any reason;

(iii) the dismissal of a batsman, except as in 9(b) above.

Law 19 – Boundaries

1. *The boundary of the field of play*

   (a) Before the toss, the umpires shall agree the boundary of the field of play with both captains. The boundary shall if possible be marked along its whole length.

   (b) The boundary shall be agreed so that no part of any sight-screen is within the field of play.

   (c) An obstacle or person within the field of play shall not be regarded as a boundary unless so decided by the umpires before the toss. See Law 3.4(ii) (To inform captains and scorers).

2. *Defining the boundary – boundary marking*

   (a) Wherever practicable the boundary shall be marked by means of a white line or a rope laid along the ground.

   (b) If the boundary is marked by a white line,

   (i) the inside edge of the line shall be the boundary edge.

   (ii) a flag, post or board used merely to highlight the position of a line marked on the ground must be placed outside the boundary edge and is not itself to be regarded as defining or marking the boundary. Note, however, the provisions of (c) below.

   (c) If a solid object is used to mark the boundary, it must have an edge or a line to constitute the boundary edge.

   (i) For a rope, which includes any similar object of curved cross section lying on the ground, the boundary edge will be the line formed by the innermost points of the rope along its length.

(ii) For a fence, which includes any similar object in contact with the ground, but with a flat surface projecting above the ground, the boundary edge will be the base line of the fence.

(d) If the boundary edge is not defined as in (b) or (c) above, the umpires and captains must agree, before the toss, what line will be the boundary edge. Where there is no physical marker for a section of boundary, the boundary edge shall be the imaginary straight line joining the two nearest marked points of the boundary edge.

(e) If a solid object used to mark the boundary is disturbed for any reason during play, then if possible it shall be restored to its original position as soon as the ball is dead. If this is not possible, then

(i) if some part of the fence or other marker has come within the field of play, that portion is to be removed from the field of play as soon as the ball is dead.

(ii) the line where the base of the fence or marker originally stood shall define the boundary edge.

3. ***Scoring a boundary***

(a) A boundary shall be scored and signalled by the umpire at the bowler's end whenever, while the ball is in play, in his opinion

(i) the ball touches the boundary, or is grounded beyond the boundary.

(ii) a fielder, with some part of his person in contact with the ball, touches the boundary or has some part of his person grounded beyond the boundary.

(b) The phrases 'touches the boundary' and 'touching the boundary' shall mean contact with either

(i) the boundary edge as defined in 2 above or

(ii) any person or obstacle within the field of play which has been desig-nated a boundary by the umpires before the toss.

(c) The phrase 'grounded beyond the boundary' shall mean contact with either

(i) any part of a line or a solid object marking the boundary, except its boundary edge or

(ii) the ground outside the boundary edge or

(iii) any object in contact with the ground outside the boundary edge.

4. **Runs allowed for boundaries**

(a) Before the toss, the umpires shall agree with both captains the runs to be allowed for boundaries. In deciding the allowances, the umpires and captains shall be guided by the prevailing custom of the ground.

(b) Unless agreed differently under (a) above, the allowances for boundaries shall be 6 runs if the ball having been struck by the bat pitches beyond the boundary, but otherwise 4 runs. These allowances shall still apply even though the ball has previously touched a fielder. See also (c) below.

(c) The ball shall be regarded as pitching beyond the boundary and 6 runs shall be scored if a fielder

(i) has any part of his person touching the boundary or grounded beyond the boundary when he catches the ball.

(ii) catches the ball and subsequently touches the boundary or grounds some part of his person beyond the boundary while carrying the ball but before completing the catch. See Law 32 (Caught).

5. **Runs scored**

When a boundary is scored,

(a) the penalty for a No ball or a Wide, if applicable, shall stand together with any penalties under any of Laws 2.6 (Player returning without permission), 18.5(b) (Deliberate short runs) or 42 (Fair and unfair play) that apply before the boundary is scored.

(b) the batting side, except in the circumstances of 6 below, shall additionally be awarded whichever is the greater of

(i) the allowance for the boundary.

(ii) the runs completed by the batsmen, together with the run in progress if they have crossed at the instant the boundary is scored.

When these runs exceed the boundary allowance, they shall replace the boundary for the purposes of Law 18.12 (Batsman returning to wicket he has left).

6.   **Overthrow or wilful act of fielder**

If the boundary results either from an overthrow or from the wilful act of a fielder the runs scored shall be

(i)   the penalty for a No ball or a Wide, if applicable, and penalties under any of Laws 2.6 (Player returning without permission), 18.5(b) (Deliberate short runs) or 42 (Fair and unfair play) that are applicable before the boundary is scored and

(ii) the allowance for the boundary and

(iii) the runs completed by the batsmen, together with the run in progress if they have crossed at the instant of the throw or act.

Law 18.12(a) (Batsman returning to wicket he has left) shall apply as from the instant of the throw or act.

Law 20 – Lost Ball

1.   **Fielder to call Lost ball**

If a ball in play cannot be found or recovered, any fielder may call Lost ball. The ball shall then become dead. See Law 23.1 (Ball is dead). Law 18.12(a) (Batsman returning to wicket he has left) shall apply as from the instant of the call.

2.   **Ball to be replaced**

The umpires shall replace the ball with one which has had wear comparable with that which the previous ball had received before it was lost or became irrecoverable. See Law 5.5 (Ball lost or becoming unfit for play).

3.   **Runs scored**

(a) The penalty for a No ball or a Wide, if applicable, shall stand, together with any penalties under any of Laws 2.6 (Player returning without permission), 18.5(b) (Deliberate short runs) or 42 (Fair and unfair play) that are applicable before the call of Lost ball.

(b) The batting side shall additionally be awarded either

(i) the runs completed by the batsmen, together with the run in progress if they have crossed at the instant of the call, or

(ii) 6 runs, whichever is the greater.

4.   *How scored*

If there is a one run penalty for a No ball or for a Wide, it shall be scored as a No ball extra or as a Wide as appropriate. See Laws 24.13 (Runs resulting from a No ball – how scored) and 25.6 (Runs resulting from a Wide – how scored). If any other penalties have been awarded to either side, they shall be scored as penalty extras. See Law 42.17 (Penalty runs). Runs to the batting side in 3(b) above shall be credited to the striker if the ball has been struck by the bat, but otherwise to the total of Byes, Leg byes, No balls or Wides as the case may be.

Law 21 – The Result

1.   *A Win – two innings match*

The side which has scored a total of runs in excess of that scored in the two completed innings of the opposing side shall win the match. Note also 6 below. A forfeited innings is to count as a completed innings. See Law 14 (Declaration and forfeiture).

2.   *A Win – one innings match*

The side which has scored in its one innings a total of runs in excess of that scored by the opposing side in its one completed innings shall win the match. Note also 6 below.

3.   *Umpires awarding a match*

(a) A match shall be lost by a side which either

(i) concedes defeat or

Law 21

(ii) in the opinion of the umpires refuses to play and the umpires shall award the match to the other side.

(b) If an umpire considers that an action by any player or players might constitute a refusal by either side to play then the umpires together shall ascertain the cause of the action. If they then decide together that this action does constitute a refusal to play by one side, they shall so inform the captain of that side. If the captain persists in the action the umpires shall award the match in accordance with (a)(ii) above.

(c) If action as in (b) above takes place after play has started and does not constitute a refusal to play

(i) playing time lost shall be counted from the start of the action until play recommences, subject to Law 15.5 (Changing agreed times for intervals).

(ii) the time for close of play on that day shall be extended by this length of time, subject to Law 3.9 (Suspension of play for adverse conditions of ground, weather or light).

(iii) if applicable, no overs shall be deducted during the last hour of the match solely on account of this time.

4. *A Tie*

The result of a match shall be a Tie when the scores are equal at the conclusion of play, but only if the side batting last has completed its innings.

5. *A Draw*

A match which is concluded, as defined in Law 16.9 (Conclusion of a match), without being determined in any of the ways stated in 1,2,3 or 4 above, shall count as a Draw.

6. *Winning hit or extras*

(a) As soon as a result is reached, as defined in 1, 2, 3 or 4 above, the match is at an end. Nothing that happens thereafter shall be regarded as part of it. Note also 9 below.

(b) The side batting last will have scored enough runs to win only if its total of runs is sufficient without including any runs completed before the dismissal of the striker by the completion of a catch or by the obstruction of a catch.

(c) If a boundary is scored before the batsmen have completed sufficient runs to win the match, then the whole of the boundary allowance shall be credited to the side's total and, in the case of a hit by the bat, to the striker's score.

7. *Statement of result*

If the side batting last wins the match, the result shall be stated as a win by the number of wickets still then to fall. If the other side wins the match, the result shall be stated as a win by runs. If the match is decided by one side conceding defeat or refusing to play, the result shall be stated as Match Conceded or Match Awarded as the case may be.

8. *Correctness of result*

Any decision as to the correctness of the scores shall be the responsibility of the umpires. See Law 3.15 (Correctness of scores).

9. *Mistakes in scoring*

If, after the umpires and players have left the field in the belief that the match has been concluded, the umpires discover that a mistake in scoring has occurred which affects the result, then, subject to 10 below, they shall adopt the following procedure.

(a) If, when the players leave the field, the side batting last has not completed its innings, and either (i) the number of overs to be bowled in the last hour has not been completed, or (ii) the agreed finishing time has not been reached, then unless one side concedes defeat the umpires shall order play to resume. If conditions permit, play will then continue until the prescribed number of overs has been completed and the time remaining has elapsed, unless a result is reached earlier. The number of overs and/or the time remaining shall be taken as they were when the players left the field; no account shall be taken of the time between that moment and the resumption of play.

(b) If, when the players leave the field, the overs have been completed and time has been reached, or if the side batting last has completed its innings, the umpires shall immediately inform both captains of the necessary corrections to the scores and to the result.

10.   *Result not to be changed*
Once the umpires have agreed with the scorers the correctness of the scores at the conclusion of the match – see Laws 3.15 (Correctness of scores) and 4.2 (Correctness of scores) – the result cannot thereafter be changed.

Law 22 – The Over

1.   *Number of balls*
The ball shall be bowled from each wicket alternately in overs of 6 balls.

2.   *Start of an over*
An over has started when the bowler starts his run up or, if he has no run up, his delivery action for the first delivery of that over.

3.   *Call of Over*
When 6 balls have been bowled other than those which are not to count in the over and as the ball becomes dead - see Law 23 (Dead ball) - the umpire shall call Over before leaving the wicket.

4.   *Balls not to count in the over*
(a) A ball shall not count as one of the 6 balls of the over unless it is delivered, even though a batsman may be dismissed or some other incident occurs before the ball is delivered.
(b) A ball which is delivered by the bowler shall not count as one of the 6 balls of the over

(i) if it is called dead, or is to be considered dead, before the striker has had an opportunity to play it. See Law 23 (Dead ball).

(ii) if it is a No ball. See Law 24 (No ball).

(iii) if it is a Wide. See Law 25 (Wide ball).

(iv) if it is called dead in the circumstances of either of Laws 23.3 (vi) (Umpire calling and signalling Dead ball) or 42.4 (Deliberate attempt to distract striker).

5. ***Umpire miscounting***

If an umpire miscounts the number of balls, the over as counted by the umpire shall stand.

6. ***Bowler changing ends***

A bowler shall be allowed to change ends as often as desired, provided only that he does not bowl two overs, or parts thereof, consecutively in the same innings.

7. ***Finishing an over***

(a) Other than at the end of an innings, a bowler shall finish an over in progress unless he is incapacitated, or he is suspended under any of Laws 17.1 (Practice on the field), 42.7 (Dangerous and unfair bowling – action by the umpire), 42.9 (Time wasting by the fielding side), or 42.12 (Bowler running on the protected area after delivering the ball).

(b) If for any reason, other than the end of an innings, an over is left uncompleted at the start of an interval or interruption of play, it shall be completed on resumption of play.

8. ***Bowler incapacitated or suspended during an over***

If for any reason a bowler is incapacitated while running up to bowl the first ball of an over, or is incapacitated or suspended during an over, the umpire shall call and signal Dead ball. Another bowler shall complete the over from the same end, provided that he does not bowl two overs, or parts thereof, consecutively in one innings.

Law 23 – Dead Ball

1. ***Ball is dead***
   (a) The ball becomes dead when
   - (i) it is finally settled in the hands of the wicket-keeper or the bowler.
   - (ii) a boundary is scored. See Law 19.3 (Scoring a boundary).
   - (iii) a batsman is dismissed.
   - (iv) whether played or not it becomes trapped between the bat and person of a batsman or between items of his clothing or equipment.
   - (v) whether played or not it lodges in the clothing or equipment of a batsman or the clothing of an umpire.
   - (vi) it lodges in a protective helmet worn by a member of the fielding side.
   - (vii) there is a contravention of either of Laws 41.2 (Fielding the ball) or 41.3 (Protective helmets belonging to the fielding side).
   - (viii) there is an award of penalty runs under Law 2.6 (Player returning without permission).
   - (ix) Lost ball is called. See Law 20 (Lost ball).
   - (x) the umpire calls Over or Time.
   (b) The ball shall be considered to be dead when it is clear to the umpire at the bowler's end that the fielding side and both batsmen at the wicket have ceased to regard it as in play.

2. ***Ball finally settled***
   Whether the ball is finally settled or not is a matter for the umpire alone to decide.

3. ***Umpire calling and signalling Dead ball***
   (a) When the ball has become dead under 1 above, the bowler's end umpire may call Dead ball, if it is necessary to inform the players.

(b) Either umpire shall call and signal Dead ball when

    (i)   he intervenes in a case of unfair play.

    (ii)   a serious injury to a player or umpire occurs.

    (iii)   he leaves his normal position for consultation.

    (iv)   one or both bails fall from the striker's wicket before he has the opportunity of playing the ball.

    (v)   he is satisfied that for an adequate reason the striker is not ready for the delivery of the ball and, if the ball is delivered, makes no attempt to play it.

    (vi)   the striker is distracted by any noise or movement or in any other way while he is preparing to receive or receiving a delivery. This shall apply whether the source of the distraction is within the game or outside it. Note, however, the provisions of Law 42.4 (Deliberate attempt to distract the striker). The ball shall not count as one of the over.

    (vii) the bowler drops the ball accidentally before delivery.

    (viii) the ball does not leave the bowler's hand for any reason other than an attempt to run out the non-striker before entering his delivery stride. See Law 42.15 (Bowler attempting to run out non-striker before delivery).

    (ix)   he is required to do so under any of the Laws.

4.   *Ball ceases to be dead*

The ball ceases to be dead – that is, it comes into play – when the bowler starts his run up or, if he has no run up, his bowling action.

5.   *Action on call of Dead ball*

(a) A ball is not to count as one of the over if it becomes dead or is to be considered dead before the striker has had an opportunity to play it.

(b) If the ball becomes dead or is to be considered dead after the striker has had an opportunity to play the ball, except in the circumstances of 3(vi) above and Law 42.4 (Deliberate attempt to distract striker), no additional delivery shall be allowed unless No ball or Wide has been called.

Law 24 – No Ball

1.   *Mode of delivery*
     (a) The umpire shall ascertain whether the bowler intends to bowl right handed or left handed, over or round the wicket, and shall so inform the striker. It is unfair if the bowler fails to notify the umpire of a change in his mode of delivery. In this case the umpire shall call and signal No ball.
     (b) Underarm bowling shall not be permitted except by special agreement before the match.

2.   *Fair delivery – the arm*
     For a delivery to be fair in respect of the arm the ball must not be thrown. See 3 below. Although it is the primary responsibility of the striker's end umpire to ensure the fairness of a delivery in this respect, there is nothing in this Law to debar the bowler's end umpire from calling and signalling No ball if he considers that the ball has been thrown.
     (a) If, in the opinion of either umpire, the ball has been thrown, he shall
         (i)   call and signal No ball.
         (ii) caution the bowler, when the ball is dead. This caution shall apply throughout the innings.
         (iii) inform the other umpire, the batsmen at the wicket, the captain of the fielding side and, as soon as practicable, the captain of the batting side of what has occurred.
     (b) If either umpire considers that after such caution a further delivery by the same bowler in that innings is thrown, the umpire concerned shall repeat the procedure set out in (a) above, indicating to the bowler that this is a final warning. This warning shall also apply throughout the innings.
     (c) If either umpire considers that a further delivery by the same bowler in that innings is thrown,
         (i)   the umpire concerned shall call and signal No ball. When the ball is dead he shall inform the other umpire, the batsmen at the wicket

and, as soon as practicable, the captain of the batting side of what has occurred.

(ii) the umpire at the bowler's end shall direct the captain of the fielding side to take the bowler off forthwith. The over shall be completed by another bowler, who shall neither have bowled the previous over nor be allowed to bowl the next over. The bowler thus taken off shall not bowl again in that innings.

(iii) the umpires together shall report the occurrence as soon as possible to the Executive of the fielding side and any Governing Body responsible for the match, who shall take such action as is considered appropriate against the captain and bowler concerned.

3.   *Definition of fair delivery – the arm*

A ball is fairly delivered in respect of the arm if, once the bowler's arm has reached the level of the shoulder in the delivery swing, the elbow joint is not straightened partially or completely from that point until the ball has left the hand. This definition shall not debar a bowler from flexing or rotating the wrist in the delivery swing.

4.   *Bowler throwing towards striker's end before delivery*

If the bowler throws the ball towards the striker's end before entering his delivery stride, either umpire shall call and signal No ball. See Law 42.16 (Batsmen stealing a run). However, the procedure stated in 2 above of caution, informing, final warning, action against the bowler and reporting shall not apply.

5.   *Fair delivery – the feet*

For a delivery to be fair in respect of the feet, in the delivery stride

(i)   the bowler's back foot must land within and not touching the return crease.

(ii) the bowler's front foot must land with some part of the foot, whether grounded or raised, behind the popping crease.

If the umpire at the bowler's end is not satisfied that both these conditions have been met, he shall call and signal No ball.

6. *Ball bouncing more than twice or rolling along the ground*
The umpire at the bowler's end shall call and signal No ball if a ball which he considers to have been delivered, without having previously touched the bat or person of the striker, either
(i) bounces more than twice or
(ii) rolls along the ground before it reaches the popping crease.

7. *Ball coming to rest in front of striker's wicket*
If a ball delivered by the bowler comes to rest in front of the line of the striker's wicket, without having touched the bat or person of the striker, the umpire shall call and signal No ball and immediately call and signal Dead ball.

8. *Call of No ball for infringement of other Laws*
In addition to the instances above, an umpire shall call and signal No ball as required by the following Laws.

Law 40.3	– Position of wicket-keeper
Law 41.5	– Limitation of on side fielders
Law 41.6	– Fielders not to encroach on the pitch
Law 42.6	– Dangerous and unfair bowling
Law 42.7	– Dangerous and unfair bowling – action by the umpire
Law 42.8	– Deliberate bowling of high full pitched balls.

9. *Revoking a call of No ball*
An umpire shall revoke the call of No ball if the ball does not leave the bowler's hand for any reason.

Law 24

10.   *No ball to over-ride Wide*

A call of No ball shall over-ride the call of Wide ball at any time. See Law 25.1 (Judging a Wide) and 25.3 (Call and signal of Wide ball).

11.   *Ball not dead*

The ball does not become dead on the call of No ball.

12.   *Penalty for a No ball*

A penalty of one run shall be awarded instantly on the call of No ball. Unless the call is revoked, this penalty shall stand even if a batsman is dismissed. It shall be in addition to any other runs scored, any boundary allowance and any other penalties awarded.

13.   *Runs resulting from a No ball – how scored*

The one run penalty for a No ball shall be scored as a No ball extra. If other penalty runs have been awarded to either side, these shall be scored as in Law 42.17 (Penalty runs). Any runs completed by the batsmen or a boundary allowance shall be credited to the striker if the ball has been struck by the bat; otherwise they also shall be scored as No ball extras.

Apart from any award of a 5 run penalty, all runs resulting from a No ball, whether as No ball extras or credited to the striker, shall be debited against the bowler.

14.   *No ball not to count*

A No ball shall not count as one of the over. See Law 22.4 (Balls not to count in the over).

15.   *Out from a No ball*

When No ball has been called, neither batsman shall be out under any of the Laws except 33 (Handled the ball), 34 (Hit the ball twice), 37 (Obstructing the field) or 38 (Run out).

Law 25 – Wide Ball

1. ### Judging a Wide
   (a) If the bowler bowls a ball, not being a No ball, the umpire shall adjudge it a Wide if according to the definition in (b) below, in his opinion, the ball passes wide of the striker where he is standing and would also have passed wide of him standing in a normal guard position.
   (b) The ball will be considered as passing wide of the striker unless it is sufficiently within his reach for him to be able to hit it with his bat by means of a normal cricket stroke.

2. ### Delivery not a Wide
   The umpire shall not adjudge a delivery as being a Wide
   (a) if the striker, by moving, either
      (i) causes the ball to pass wide of him, as defined in 1(b) above or
      (ii) brings the ball sufficiently within his reach to be able to hit it with his bat by means of a normal cricket stroke.
   (b) if the ball touches the striker's bat or person.

3. ### Call and signal of Wide ball
   (a) If the umpire adjudges a delivery to be a Wide he shall call and signal Wide ball as soon as the ball passes the striker's wicket. It shall, however, be considered to have been a Wide from the instant of delivery, even though it cannot be called Wide until it passes the striker's wicket.
   (b) The umpire shall revoke the call of Wide ball if there is then any contact between the ball and the striker's bat or person.
   (c) The umpire shall revoke the call of Wide ball if a delivery is called a No ball. See Law 24.10 (No ball to over-ride Wide).

4. ### Ball not dead
   The ball does not become dead on the call of Wide ball.

5. ***Penalty for a Wide***

A penalty of one run shall be awarded instantly on the call of Wide ball. Unless the call is revoked (see 3 above), this penalty shall stand even if a batsman is dismissed, and shall be in addition to any other runs scored, any boundary allowance and any other penalties awarded.

6. ***Runs resulting from a Wide – how scored***

All runs completed by the batsmen or a boundary allowance, together with the penalty for the Wide, shall be scored as Wide balls. Apart from any award of a 5 run penalty, all runs resulting from a Wide ball shall be debited against the bowler.

7. ***Wide not to count***

A Wide shall not count as one of the over. See Law 22.4 (Balls not to count in the over).

8. ***Out from a Wide***

When Wide ball has been called, neither batsman shall be out under any of the Laws except 33 (Handled the ball), 35 (Hit wicket), 37 (Obstructing the field), 38 (Run out) or 39 (Stumped).

Law 26 – Bye and Leg Bye

1. ***Byes***

If the ball, not being a No ball or a Wide, passes the striker without touching his bat or person, any runs completed by the batsmen or a boundary allowance shall be credited as Byes to the batting side.

2. ***Leg byes***

(a) If the ball, not having previously touched the striker's bat, strikes his person and the umpire is satisfied that the striker has either

(i) attempted to play the ball with his bat, or

(ii) tried to avoid being hit by the ball,

then any runs completed by the batsmen or a boundary allowance shall be credited to the batting side as Leg byes, unless No ball has been called.

(b) If No ball has been called, the runs in (a) above, together with the penalty for the No ball, shall be scored as No ball extras.

3. *Leg byes not to be awarded*

If in the circumstances of 2(a) above, the umpire considers that neither of the conditions (i) and (ii) has been met, then Leg byes will not be awarded. The batting side shall not be credited with any runs from that delivery apart from the.39 one run penalty for a No ball if applicable. Moreover, no other penalties shall be awarded to the batting side when the ball is dead. See Law 42.17 (Penalty runs). The following procedure shall be adopted.

(a) If no run is attempted but the ball reaches the boundary, the umpire shall call and signal Dead ball, and disallow the boundary.

(b) If runs are attempted and if

(i) neither batsman is dismissed and the ball does not become dead for any other reason, the umpire shall call and signal Dead ball as soon as one run is completed or the ball reaches the boundary. The batsmen shall return to their original ends. The run or boundary shall be disallowed.

(ii) before one run is completed or the ball reaches the boundary, a batsman is dismissed, or the ball becomes dead for any other reason, all the provisions of the Laws will apply, except that no runs and no penalties shall be credited to the batting side, other than the penalty for a No ball if applicable.

Law 27 – Appeals

1. *Umpire not to give batsman out without an appeal*

Neither umpire shall give a batsman out, even though he may be out under the Laws, unless appealed to by the fielding side. This shall not debar a batsman who is out under any of the Laws from leaving his wicket without an appeal having been made. Note, however, the provisions of 7 below.

2. *Batsman dismissed*

A batsman is dismissed if either

(a) he is given out by an umpire, on appeal or

(b) he is out under any of the Laws and leaves his wicket as in 1 above.

3. *Timing of appeals*

For an appeal to be valid it must be made before the bowler begins his run up or, if he has no run up, his bowling action to deliver the next ball, and before Time has been called.

The call of Over does not invalidate an appeal made prior to the start of the following over provided Time has not been called. See Laws 16.2 (Call of Time) and 22.2 (Start of an over).

4. *Appeal 'How's That?'*

An appeal 'How's That?' covers all ways of being out.

5. *Answering appeals*

The umpire at the bowler's end shall answer all appeals except those arising out of any of Laws 35 (Hit wicket), 39 (Stumped) or 38 (Run out) when this occurs at the striker's wicket. A decision Not out by one umpire shall not prevent the other umpire from giving a decision, provided that each is considering only matters within his jurisdiction.

When a batsman has been given Not out, either umpire may, within his jurisdiction, answer a further appeal provided that it is made in accordance with 3 above.

6. *Consultation by umpires*

Each umpire shall answer appeals on matters within his own jurisdiction. If an umpire is doubtful about any point that the other umpire may have been in a better position to see, he shall consult the latter on this point of fact and shall then give his decision. If, after consultation, there is still doubt remaining the decision shall be Not out.

7. *Batsman leaving his wicket under a misapprehension*
    An umpire shall intervene if satisfied that a batsman, not having been given out, has left his wicket under a misapprehension that he is out. The umpire intervening shall call and signal Dead ball to prevent any further action by the fielding side and shall recall the batsman.

8. *Withdrawal of an appeal*
    The captain of the fielding side may withdraw an appeal only with the consent of the umpire within whose jurisdiction the appeal falls and before the outgoing batsman has left the field of play. If such consent is given the umpire concerned shall, if applicable, revoke his decision and recall the batsman.

9. *Umpire's decision*
    An umpire may alter his decision provided that such alteration is made promptly. This apart, an umpire's decision, once made, is final.

Law 28 – The Wicket is Down

1. *Wicket put down*
    (a) The wicket is put down if a bail is completely removed from the top of the stumps, or a stump is struck out of the ground by
    (i)   the ball.
    (ii) the striker's bat, whether he is holding it or has let go of it.
    (iii) the striker's person or by any part of his clothing or equipment becoming detached from his person.
    (iii) a fielder, with his hand or arm, providing that the ball is held in the

hand or hands so used, or in the hand of the arm so used. The wicket is also put down if a fielder pulls a stump out of the ground in the same manner.

(b) The disturbance of a bail, whether temporary or not, shall not constitute its complete removal from the top of the stumps, but if a bail in falling lodges between two of the stumps this shall be regarded as complete removal.

2. **One bail off**

If one bail is off, it shall be sufficient for the purpose of putting the wicket down to remove the remaining bail, or to strike or pull any of the three stumps out of the ground, in any of the ways stated in 1 above.

3. **Remaking the wicket**

If the wicket is broken or put down while the ball is in play, the umpire shall not remake the wicket until the ball is dead. See Law 23 (Dead ball). Any fielder, however, may

(i) replace a bail or bails on top of the stumps.

(ii) put back one or more stumps into the ground where the wicket originally stood.

4. **Dispensing with bails**

If the umpires have agreed to dispense with bails, in accordance with Law 8.5 (Dispensing with bails), the decision as to whether the wicket has been put down is one for the umpire concerned to decide.

(a) After a decision to play without bails, the wicket has been put down if the umpire concerned is satisfied that the wicket has been struck by the ball, by the striker's bat, person, or items of his clothing or equipment separated from his person as described in 1(a)(ii) or 1(a)(iii) above, or by a fielder with the hand holding the ball or with the arm of the hand holding the ball.

(b) If the wicket has already been broken or put down, (a) above shall apply to any stump or stumps still in the ground. Any fielder may replace a stump or stumps, in accordance with 3 above, in order to have an opportunity of putting the wicket down.

Law 29 – Batsman Out of His Ground

1. ### *When out of his ground*
   A batsman shall be considered to be out of his ground unless his bat or some part of his person is grounded behind the popping crease at that end.

2. ### *Which is a batsman's ground*
   (a) If only one batsman is within a ground
   - (i) it is his ground.
   - (ii) it remains his ground even if he is later joined there by the other batsman.

   (b) If both batsmen are in the same ground and one of them subsequently leaves it, (a)(i) above applies.

   (c) If there is no batsman in either ground, then each ground belongs to whichever of the batsmen is nearer to it, or, if the batsmen are level, to whichever was nearer to it immediately prior to their drawing level.

   (d) If a ground belongs to one batsman, then, unless there is a striker with a runner, the other ground belongs to the other batsman irrespective of his position.

   (e) When a batsman with a runner is striker, his ground is always that at the wicket-keeper's end. However, (a), (b), (c) and (d) above will still apply, but only to the runner and the non-striker, so that that ground will also belong to either the non-striker or the runner, as the case may be.

3. ### *Position of non-striker*
   The non-striker when standing at the bowler's end, should be positioned on

the opposite side of the wicket to that from which the ball is being delivered, unless a request to do otherwise is granted by the umpire.

Law 30 – Bowled

1. ### *Out Bowled*
   (a) The striker is out Bowled if his wicket is put down by a ball delivered by the bowler, not being a No ball, even if it first touches his bat or person.
   (b) Notwithstanding (a) above he shall not be out Bowled if before striking the wicket the ball has been in contact with any other player or with an umpire. He will, however, be subject to Laws 33 (Handled the ball), 37 (Obstructing the field), 38 (Run out) and 39 (Stumped).

2. ### *Bowled to take precedence*
   The striker is out Bowled if his wicket is put down as in 1 above, even though a decision against him for any other method of dismissal would be justified.

Law 31 – Timed Out

1. ### *Out Timed out*
   (a) Unless Time has been called, the incoming batsman must be in position to take guard or for his partner to be ready to receive the next ball within 3 minutes of the fall of the previous wicket. If this requirement is not met, the incoming batsman will be out, Timed out.
   (b) In the event of protracted delay in which no batsman comes to the wicket, the umpires shall adopt the procedure of Law 21.3 (Umpires awarding a match). For the purposes of that Law the start of the action shall be taken as the expiry of the 3 minutes referred to above.

2.   *Bowler does not get credit*

The bowler does not get credit for the wicket.

Law 32 – Caught

1.   *Out Caught*

The striker is out Caught if a ball delivered by the bowler, not being a No ball, touches his bat without having previously been in contact with any member of the fielding side and is subsequently held by a fielder as a fair catch before it touches the ground.

2.   *Caught to take precedence*

If the criteria of 1 above are met and the striker is not out Bowled, then he is out Caught, even though a decision against either batsman for another method of dismissal would be justified. Runs completed by the batsmen before the completion of the catch will not be scored. Note also Laws 21.6 (Winning hit or extras) and 42.17(b) (Penalty runs).

3.   *A fair catch*

A catch shall be considered to have been fairly made if

(a) throughout the act of making the catch

    (i) any fielder in contact with the ball is within the field of play. See 4 below.

    (ii) the ball is at no time in contact with any object grounded beyond the boundary.

The act of making the catch shall start from the time when a fielder first handles the ball and shall end when a fielder obtains complete control both over the ball and over his own movement.

(b) the ball is hugged to the body of the catcher or accidentally lodges in his clothing or, in the case of the wicket-keeper, in his pads. However, it is not a fair catch if the ball lodges in a protective helmet worn by a fielder. See Law 23 (Dead ball).

(c) the ball does not touch the ground, even though the hand holding it does so in effecting the catch.

(d) a fielder catches the ball after it has been lawfully struck more than once by the striker, but only if the ball has not touched the ground since first being struck.

(e) a fielder catches the ball after it has touched an umpire, another fielder or the other batsman. However, it is not a fair catch if the ball has touched a protective helmet worn by a fielder, although the ball remains in play.

(f) a fielder catches the ball in the air after it has crossed the boundary provided that

   (i) he has no part of his person touching, or grounded beyond, the boundary at any time when he is in contact with the ball.

   (ii) the ball has not been grounded beyond the boundary. See Law 19.3 (Scoring a boundary).

(g) the ball is caught off an obstruction within the boundary, provided it has not previously been decided to regard the obstruction as a boundary.

4.   *Fielder within the field of play*

(a) A fielder is not within the field of play if he touches the boundary or has any part of his person grounded beyond the boundary. See Law 19.3 (Scoring a Boundary)

(b) 6 runs shall be scored if a fielder

   (i) has any part of his person touching, or grounded beyond, the boundary when he catches the ball.

   (ii) catches the ball and subsequently touches the boundary or grounds some part of his person over the boundary while carrying the ball but before completing the catch. See Laws 19.3 (Scoring a boundary) and 19.4 (Runs allowed for boundaries).

5.   *No runs to be scored*

If the striker is dismissed Caught, runs from that delivery completed by the batsmen before the completion of the catch shall not be scored, but any penalties awarded to either side when the ball is dead, if applicable, will stand. Law 18.12(a) (Batsman returning to wicket he has left) shall apply from the instant of the catch.

Law 33 – Handled the Ball

1.   *Out Handled the ball*

Either batsman is out Handled the ball if he wilfully touches the ball while in play with a hand or hands not holding the bat unless he does so with the consent of the opposing side.

2.   *Not out Handled the ball*

Notwithstanding 1 above, a batsman will not be out under this Law if
  (i) he handles the ball in order to avoid injury.
  (ii) he uses his hand or hands to return the ball to any member of the fielding side without the consent of that side. Note, however, the provisions of Law 37.4 (Returning the ball to a member of the fielding side).

3.   *Runs scored*

If either batsman is dismissed under this Law, any runs completed before the offence, together with any penalty extras and the penalty for a No ball or Wide, if applicable, shall be scored. See Laws 18.10 (Runs scored when a batsman is dismissed) and 42.17 (Penalty runs).

4.   *Bowler does not get credit*

The bowler does not get credit for the wicket.

Law 34 – Hit the Ball Twice

1.   *Out Hit the ball twice*

(a) The striker is out Hit the ball twice if, while the ball is in play, it strikes any part of his person or is struck by his bat and, before the ball has been touched by a fielder, he wilfully strikes it again with his bat or person, other than a hand not holding the bat, except for the sole purpose of guarding his wicket. See 3 below and Laws 33 (Handled the ball) and 37 (Obstructing the field).

(b) For the purpose of this Law, 'struck' or 'strike' shall include contact with the person of the striker.

2. *Not out Hit the ball twice*

Notwithstanding 1(a) above, the striker will not be out under this Law if

(i) he makes a second or subsequent stroke in order to return the ball to any member of the fielding side. Note, however, the provisions of Law 37.4 (Returning the ball to a member of the fielding side).

(ii) he wilfully strikes the ball after it has touched a fielder. Note, however, the provisions of Law 37.1 (Out Obstructing the field).

3. *Ball lawfully struck more than once*

Solely in order to guard his wicket and before the ball has been touched by a fielder, the striker may lawfully strike the ball more than once with his bat or with any part of his person other than a hand not holding the bat.

Notwithstanding this provision, the striker may not prevent the ball from being caught by making more than one stroke in defence of his wicket. See Law 37.3 (Obstructing a ball from being caught).

4. *Runs permitted from ball lawfully struck more than once*

When the ball is lawfully struck more than once, as permitted in 3 above, only the first strike is to be considered in determining whether runs are to be allowed and how they are to be scored.

(a) If on the first strike the umpire is satisfied that either

(i) the ball first struck the bat or

(ii) the striker attempted to play the ball with his bat or

(iii) the striker tried to avoid being hit by the ball then any penalties to the batting side that are applicable shall be allowed.

Law 34

(b) If the conditions in (a) above are met then, if they result from overthrows, and only if they result from overthrows, runs completed by the batsmen or a boundary will be allowed in addition to any penalties that are applicable. They shall be credited to the striker if the first strike was with the bat. If the first strike was on the person of the striker they shall be scored as Leg byes or No ball extras, as appropriate. See Law 26.2 (Leg byes).

(c) If the conditions of (a) above are met and there is no overthrow until after the batsmen have started to run, but before one run is completed,

(i) only subsequent completed runs or a boundary shall be allowed. The first run shall count as a completed run for this purpose only if the batsmen have not crossed at the instant of the throw.

(ii) if in these circumstances the ball goes to the boundary from the throw then, notwithstanding the provisions of Law 19.6 (Overthrow or wilful act of fielder), only the boundary allowance shall be scored.

(iii) if the ball goes to the boundary as the result of a further overthrow, then runs completed by the batsmen after the first throw and before this final throw shall be added to the boundary allowance. The run in progress at the first throw will count only if they have not crossed at that moment; the run in progress at the final throw shall count only if they have crossed at that moment. Law 18.12 (Batsman returning to wicket he has left) shall apply as from the moment of the final throw.

(d) If, in the opinion of the umpire, none of the conditions in (a) above have been met then, whether there is an overthrow or not, the batting side shall not be credited with any runs from that delivery apart from the penalty for a No ball if applicable. Moreover, no other penalties shall be awarded to the batting side when the ball is dead. See Law 42.17 (Penalty runs).

5.   *Ball lawfully struck more than once – action by the umpire*

If no runs are to be allowed, either in the circumstances of 4(d) above, or because there has been no overthrow and

(a) if no run is attempted but the ball reaches the boundary, the umpire shall call and signal Dead ball and disallow the boundary.

(b) if the batsmen run and

    (i) neither batsman is dismissed and the ball does not become dead for any other reason, the umpire shall call and signal Dead ball as soon as one run is completed or the ball reaches the boundary. The batsmen shall return to their original ends. The run or boundary shall be disallowed.

    (ii) a batsman is dismissed, or if for any other reason the ball becomes dead before one run is completed or the ball reaches the boundary, all the provisions of the Laws will apply except that the award of penalties to the batting side shall be as laid down in 4(a) or 4(d) above as appropriate.

6.   *Bowler does not get credit*

The bowler does not get credit for the wicket.

Law 35 – Hit Wicket

1.   *Out Hit wicket*

The striker is out Hit wicket if, while the ball is in play, his wicket is put down either by the striker's bat or person as described in Law 28.1(a)(ii) and (iii) (Wicket put down) either

(i) in the course of any action taken by him in preparing to receive or in receiving a delivery, or

(ii) in setting off for his first run immediately after playing, or playing at, the ball, or

(iii) if he makes no attempt to play the ball, in setting off for his first run, providing that in the opinion of the umpire this is immediately after he has had the opportunity of playing the ball, or

(iv) in lawfully making a second or further stroke for the purpose of guarding his wicket within the provisions of Law 34.3 (Ball lawfully struck more than once).

2.   **Not out Hit wicket**

Notwithstanding 1 above, the batsman is not out under this Law should his wicket be put down in any of the ways referred to in 1 above if

(a) it occurs after he has completed any action in receiving the delivery, other than as in 1(ii), (iii) or (iv) above.

(b) it occurs when he is in the act of running, other than in setting off immediately for his first run.

(c) it occurs when he is trying to avoid being run out or stumped.

(d) it occurs while he is trying to avoid a throw-in at any time.

(e) the bowler after starting his run up, or his bowling action if he has no run up, does not deliver the ball. In this case either umpire shall immediately call and signal Dead ball. See Law 23.3 (Umpire calling and signalling Dead ball).

(f) the delivery is a No ball.

Law 36 – Leg Before Wicket

1.   **Out LBW**

The striker is out LBW in the circumstances set out below.

(a) The bowler delivers a ball, not being a No ball and

(b) the ball, if it is not intercepted full pitch, pitches in line between wicket and wicket or on the off side of the striker's wicket and

(c) the ball not having previously touched his bat, the striker intercepts the ball, either full-pitch or after pitching, with any part of his person and

(d) the point of impact, even if above the level of the bails, either

(i) is between wicket and wicket or

(ii) is either between wicket and wicket or outside the line of the off stump, if the striker has made no genuine attempt to play the ball with his bat and

(e) but for the interception, the ball would have hit the wicket.

2.   *Interception of the ball*

(a) In assessing points (c), (d) and (e) in 1 above, only the first interception is to be considered.

(b) In assessing point (e) in 1 above, it is to be assumed that the path of the ball before interception would have continued after interception, irrespective of whether the ball might have pitched subsequently or not.

3.   *Off side of wicket*

The off side of the striker's wicket shall be determined by the striker's stance at the moment the ball comes into play for that delivery.

Law 37 – Obstructing the Field

1.   *Out Obstructing the field*

Either batsman is out Obstructing the field if he wilfully obstructs or distracts the opposing side by word or action. It shall be regarded as obstruction if either batsman wilfully, and without the consent of the fielding side, strikes the ball with his bat or person, other than a hand not holding the bat, after the ball has touched a fielder. See 4 below.

2.   *Accidental obstruction*

It is for either umpire to decide whether any obstruction or distraction is wilful or not. He shall consult the other umpire if he has any doubt.

3.   *Obstructing a ball from being caught*

The striker is out should wilful obstruction or distraction by either batsman prevent a catch being made.

This shall apply even though the striker causes the obstruction in lawfully guarding his wicket under the provisions of Law 34.3 (Ball lawfully struck more than once).

4. ***Returning the ball to a member of the fielding side***
Either batsman is out under this Law if, without the consent of the fielding side and while the ball is in play, he uses his bat or person to return the ball to any member of that side.

5. ***Runs scored***
If a batsman is dismissed under this Law, runs completed by the batsmen before the offence shall be scored, together with the penalty for a No ball or a Wide, if applicable. Other penalties that may be awarded to either side when the ball is dead shall also stand. See Law 42.17(b) (Penalty runs).

If, however, the obstruction prevents a catch from being made, runs completed by the batsmen before the offence shall not be scored, but other penalties that may be awarded to either side when the ball is dead shall stand. See Law 42.17(b) (Penalty runs).

6. ***Bowler does not get credit***
The bowler does not get credit for the wicket.

Law 38 – Run Out

1. ***Out Run out***
(a) Either batsman is out Run out, except as in 2 below, if at any time while the ball is in play
  (i) he is out of his ground and
  (ii) his wicket is fairly put down by the opposing side.
(b) (a) above shall apply even though No ball has been called and whether or not a run is being attempted, except in the circumstances of Law 39.3(b) (Not out Stumped).

2. ***Batsman not Run out***
Notwithstanding 1 above, a batsman is not out Run out if

(a) he has been within his ground and has subsequently left it to avoid injury, when the wicket is put down.

(b) the ball has not subsequently been touched again by a fielder, after the bowler has entered his delivery stride, before the wicket is put down.

(c) the ball, having been played by the striker, or having come off his person, directly strikes a helmet worn by a fielder and without further contact with him or any other fielder rebounds directly on to the wicket. However, the ball remains in play and either batsman may be Run out in the circumstances of 1 above if a wicket is subsequently put down.

(d) he is out Stumped. See Law 39.1(b) (Out Stumped).

(e) he is out of his ground, not attempting a run and his wicket is fairly put down by the wicket-keeper without the intervention of another member of the fielding side, if No ball has been called. See Law 39.3(b) (Not out Stumped).

3.   *Which batsman is out*

The batsman out in the circumstances of 1 above is the one whose ground is at the end where the wicket is put down. See Laws 2.8 (Transgression of the Laws by a batsman who has a runner) and 29.2 (Which is a batsman's ground).

4.   *Runs scored*

If a batsman is dismissed Run out, the batting side shall score the runs completed before the dismissal, together with the penalty for a No ball or a Wide, if applicable. Other penalties to either side that may be awarded when the ball is dead shall also stand. See Law 42.17 (Penalty runs).

If, however, a striker with a runner is himself dismissed Run out, runs completed by the runner and the other batsman before the dismissal shall not be scored. The penalty for a No ball or a Wide and any other penalties to either side that may be awarded when the ball is dead shall stand. See Laws 2.8 (Transgression of the Laws by a batsman who has a runner) and 42.17(b) (Penalty runs).

5.   *Bowler does not get credit*
        The bowler does not get credit for the wicket.

Law 39 – Stumped

1.   *Out Stumped*
        (a) The striker is out Stumped if
            (i)   he is out of his ground and
            (ii) he is receiving a ball which is not a No ball and
            (iii) he is not attempting a run and
            (iv) his wicket is put down by the wicket-keeper without the intervention
                  of another member of the fielding side. Note Law 40.3 (Position of
                  wicket-keeper).
        (b) The striker is out Stumped if all the conditions of (a) above are satisfied,
            even though a decision of Run out would be justified.

2.   *Ball rebounding from wicket-keeper's person*
        (a) If the wicket is put down by the ball, it shall be regarded as having been
            put down by the wicket-keeper if the ball
            (i)   rebounds on to the stumps from any part of his person or equipment,
                  other than a protective helmet or
            (ii) has been kicked or thrown on to the stumps by the wicket-keeper.
        (b) If the ball touches a helmet worn by the wicket-keeper, the ball is still in
            play but the striker shall not be out Stumped. He will, however, be liable to
            be Run out in these circumstances if there is subsequent contact between
            the ball and any member of the fielding side. Note, however, 3 below.

3.   *Not out Stumped*
        (a) If the striker is not out Stumped, he is liable to be out Run out if the
            conditions of Law 38 (Run out) apply, except as set out in (b) below.
        (b) The striker shall not be out Run out if he is out of his ground, not attempting

a run, and his wicket is fairly put down by the wicket-keeper without the intervention of another member of the fielding side, if No ball has been called.

Law 40 – The Wicket-Keeper

1.   *Protective equipment*
The wicket-keeper is the only member of the fielding side permitted to wear gloves and external leg guards. If he does so, these are to be regarded as part of his person for the purposes of Law 41.2 (Fielding the ball). If by his actions and positioning it is apparent to the umpires that he will not be able to discharge his duties as a wicket-keeper, he shall forfeit this right and also the right to be recognised as a wicket-keeper for the purposes of Laws 32.3 (A fair catch), 39 (Stumped), 41.1 (Protective equipment), 41.5 (Limitation of on side fielders) and 41.6 (Fielders not to encroach on the pitch).

2.   *Gloves*
If the wicket-keeper wears gloves as permitted under 1 above, they shall have no webbing between fingers except that a single piece of flat non-stretch material may be inserted between index finger and thumb solely as a means of support. This insert shall not form a pouch when the hand is extended. See Appendix C.

3.   *Position of wicket-keeper*
The wicket-keeper shall remain wholly behind the wicket at the striker's end from the moment the ball comes into play until
(a) a ball delivered by the bowler either
   (i) touches the bat or person of the striker or
   (ii) passes the wicket at the striker's end or
(b) the striker attempts a run.
In the event of the wicket-keeper contravening this Law, the umpire at the

striker's end shall call and signal No ball as soon as possible after the delivery of the ball.

4. *Movement by wicket-keeper*
It is unfair if a wicket-keeper standing back makes a significant movement towards the wicket after the ball comes into play and before it reaches the striker. In the event of such unfair movement by the wicket-keeper, either umpire shall call and signal Dead ball. It will not be considered a significant movement if the wicket-keeper moves a few paces forward for a slower delivery.

5. *Restriction on actions of wicket-keeper*
If the wicket-keeper interferes with the striker's right to play the ball and to guard his wicket, the striker shall not be out, except under Laws 33 (Handled the ball), 34 (Hit the ball twice), 37 (Obstructing the field) or 38 (Run out).

6. *Interference with wicket-keeper by striker*
If, in playing at the ball or in the legitimate defence of his wicket, the striker interferes with the wicket-keeper, he shall not be out, except as provided for in Law 37.3 (Obstructing a ball from being caught).

Law 41 – The Fielder

1. *Protective equipment*
No member of the fielding side other than the wicket-keeper shall be permitted to wear gloves or external leg guards. In addition, protection for the hand or fingers may be worn only with the consent of the umpires.

2. *Fielding the ball*
A fielder may field the ball with any part of his person but if, while the ball is in play he wilfully fields it otherwise,

(a) the ball shall become dead and 5 penalty runs shall be awarded to the batting side. See Law 42.17 (Penalty runs).

(b) the umpire shall inform the other umpire, the captain of the fielding side, the batsmen and, as soon as practicable, the captain of the batting side of what has occurred.

(c) the umpires together shall report the occurrence as soon as possible to the Executive of the fielding side and any Governing Body responsible for the match who shall take such action as is considered appropriate against the captain and player concerned.

3.   *Protective helmets belonging to the fielding side*

Protective helmets, when not in use by fielders, shall only be placed, if above the surface, on the ground behind the wicket-keeper and in line with both sets of stumps. If a helmet belonging to the fielding side is on the ground within the field of play, and the ball while in play strikes it, the ball shall become dead. 5 penalty runs shall then be awarded to the batting side. See Laws 18.11 (Runs scored when ball becomes dead) and 42.17 (Penalty runs).

4.   *Penalty runs not to be awarded*

Notwithstanding 2 and 3 above, if from the delivery by the bowler the ball first struck the person of the striker and if, in the opinion of the umpire, the striker neither

(i) attempted to play the ball with his bat, nor

(ii) tried to avoid being hit by the ball,

then no award of 5 penalty runs shall be made and no other runs or penalties shall be credited to the batting side except the penalty for a No ball if applicable. See Law 26.3 (Leg byes not to be awarded).

5.   *Limitation of on side fielders*

At the instant of the bowler's delivery there shall not be more than two fielders, other than the wicket-keeper, behind the popping crease on the on side. A fielder will be considered to be behind the popping crease unless the whole of his person, whether grounded or in the air, is in front of this line.

In the event of infringement of this Law by the fielding side, the umpire at the striker's end shall call and signal No ball.

6.   *Fielders not to encroach on the pitch*
While the ball is in play and until the ball has made contact with the bat or person of the striker, or has passed the striker's bat, no fielder, other than the bowler, may have any part of his person grounded on or extended over the pitch.

In the event of infringement of this Law by any fielder other than the wicket-keeper, the umpire at the bowler's end shall call and signal No ball as soon as possible after the delivery of the ball. Note, however, Law 40.3 (Position of wicket-keeper).

7.   *Movement by fielders*
Any significant movement by any fielder after the ball comes into play and before the ball reaches the striker is unfair. In the event of such unfair movement, either umpire shall call and signal Dead ball. Note also the provisions of Law 42.4 (Deliberate attempt to distract striker).

8.   *Definition of significant movement*
(a) For close fielders anything other than minor adjustments to stance or position in relation to the striker is significant.
(b) In the outfield, fielders are permitted to move in towards the striker or striker's wicket, provided that 5 above is not contravened. Anything other than slight movement off line or away from the striker is to be considered significant.
(c) For restrictions on movement by the wicket-keeper see Law 40.4 (Movement by wicket-keeper).

Law 42 – Fair and Unfair Play

1. *Fair and unfair play – responsibility of captains*

   The responsibility lies with the captains for ensuring that play is conducted within the spirit and traditions of the game, as described in The Preamble – The Spirit of Cricket, as well as within the Laws.

2. *Fair and unfair play – responsibility of umpires*

   The umpires shall be the sole judges of fair and unfair play. If either umpire considers an action, not covered by the Laws, to be unfair, he shall intervene without appeal and, if the ball is in play, shall call and signal Dead ball and implement the procedure as set out in 18 below. Otherwise the umpires shall not interfere with the progress of play, except as required to do so by the Laws.

3. *The match ball – changing its condition*

   (a) Any fielder may
       (i) polish the ball provided that no artificial substance is used and that such polishing wastes no time.
       (ii) remove mud from the ball under the supervision of the umpire.
       (iii) dry a wet ball on a towel.
   (b) It is unfair for anyone to rub the ball on the ground for any reason, interfere with any of the seams or the surface of the ball, use any implement, or take any other action whatsoever which is likely to alter the condition of the ball, except as permitted in (a) above.
   (c) The umpires shall make frequent and irregular inspections of the ball.
   (d) In the event of any fielder changing the condition of the ball unfairly, as set out in (b) above, the umpires after consultation shall
       (i) change the ball forthwith. It shall be for the umpires to decide on the replacement ball, which shall, in their opinion, have had wear comparable with that which the previous ball had received immediately prior to the contravention.

(ii) inform the batsmen that the ball has been changed.

(iii) award 5 penalty runs to the batting side. See 17 below.

(iv) inform the captain of the fielding side that the reason for the action was the unfair interference with the ball.

(v) inform the captain of the batting side as soon as practicable of what has occurred.

(vi) report the occurrence as soon as possible to the Executive of the fielding side and any Governing Body responsible for the match, who shall take such action as is considered appropriate against the captain and team concerned.

(e) If there is any further instance of unfairly changing the condition of the ball in that innings, the umpires after consultation shall

(i) repeat the procedure in (d)(i), (ii) and (iii) above.

(ii) inform the captain of the fielding side of the reason for the action taken and direct him to take off forthwith the bowler who delivered the immediately preceding ball. The bowler thus taken off shall not be allowed to bowl again in that innings.

(iii) inform the captain of the batting side as soon as practicable of what has occurred.

(iv) report this further occurrence as soon as possible to the Executive of the fielding side and any Governing Body responsible for the match, who shall take such action as is considered appropriate against the captain and team concerned.

4.   *Deliberate attempt to distract striker*

It is unfair for any member of the fielding side deliberately to attempt to distract the striker while he is preparing to receive or receiving a delivery.

(a) If either umpire considers that any action by a member of the fielding side is such an attempt, at the first instance he shall

(i) immediately call and signal Dead ball.

(ii) warn the captain of the fielding side that the action is unfair and indicate that this is a first and final warning.

Law 42

(iii) inform the other umpire and the batsmen of what has occurred.

Neither batsman shall be dismissed from that delivery and the ball shall not count as one of the over.

(b) If there is any further such deliberate attempt in that innings, by any member of the fielding side, the procedures, other than warning, as set out in (a) above shall apply. Additionally, the umpire at the bowler's end shall

(i) award 5 penalty runs to the batting side. See 17 below.

(ii) inform the captain of the fielding side of the reason for this action and, as soon as practicable, inform the captain of the batting side.

(iii) report the occurrence, together with the other umpire, as soon as possible to the Executive of the fielding side and any Governing Body responsible for the match, who shall take such action as is considered appropriate against the captain and player or players concerned.

5.   *Deliberate distraction or obstruction of batsman*

In addition to 4 above, it is unfair for any member of the fielding side, by word or action, wilfully to attempt to distract or to obstruct either batsman after the striker has received the ball.

(a) It is for either one of the umpires to decide whether any distraction or obstruction is wilful or not.

(b) If either umpire considers that a member of the fielding side has wilfully caused or attempted to cause such a distraction or obstruction he shall

(i) immediately call and signal Dead ball.

(ii) inform the captain of the fielding side and the other umpire of the reason for the call.

Additionally,

(iii) neither batsman shall be dismissed from that delivery.

(iv) 5 penalty runs shall be awarded to the batting side. See 17 below. In this instance, the run in progress shall be scored, whether or not the batsmen had crossed at the instant of the call. See Law 18.11 (Runs scored when ball becomes dead).

(v) the umpire at the bowler's end shall inform the captain of the fielding side of the reason for this action and, as soon as practicable, inform the captain of the batting side.

(vi) the umpires shall report the occurrence as soon as possible to the Executive of the fielding side and any Governing Body responsible for the match, who shall take such action as is considered appropriate against the captain and player or players concerned.

6.   *Dangerous and unfair bowling*

(a) Bowling of fast short pitched balls

(i) The bowling of fast short pitched balls is dangerous and unfair if the umpire at the bowler's end considers that by their repetition and taking into account their length, height and direction they are likely to inflict physical injury on the striker, irrespective of the protective equipment he may be wearing. The relative skill of the striker shall be taken into consideration.

(ii) Any delivery which, after pitching, passes or would have passed over head height of the striker standing upright at the crease, although not threatening physical injury, is unfair and shall be considered as part of the repetition sequence in (i) above.

The umpire shall call and signal No ball for each such delivery.

(b) Bowling of high full pitched balls

(i) Any delivery, other than a slow paced one, which passes or would have passed on the full above waist height of the striker standing upright at the crease is to be deemed dangerous and unfair, whether or not it is likely to inflict physical injury on the striker.

(ii) A slow delivery which passes or would have passed on the full above shoulder height of the striker standing upright at the crease is to be deemed dangerous and unfair, whether or not it is likely to inflict physical injury on the striker.

7.   *Dangerous and unfair bowling – action by the umpire*

(a) In the event of dangerous and/or unfair bowling, as defined in 6 above, by any bowler, except as in 8 below, at the first instance the umpire at the bowler's end shall call and signal No ball and, when the ball is dead, caution the bowler, inform the other umpire, the captain of the fielding side and the batsmen of what has occurred. This caution shall continue to apply throughout the innings.

(b) If there is a second instance of such dangerous and/or unfair bowling by the same bowler in that innings, the umpire at the bowler's end shall repeat the above procedure and indicate to the bowler that this is a final warning. Both the above caution and final warning shall continue to apply even though the bowler may later change ends.

(c) Should there be a further instance by the same bowler in that innings, the umpire shall

(i) call and signal No ball.

(ii) direct the captain, when the ball is dead, to take the bowler off forthwith. The over shall be completed by another bowler, who shall neither have bowled the previous over nor be allowed to bowl the next over.

The bowler thus taken off shall not be allowed to bowl again in that innings.

(iii) report the occurrence to the other umpire, the batsmen and, as soon as practicable, the captain of the batting side.

(iv) report the occurrence, with the other umpire, as soon as possible to the Executive of the fielding side and to any Governing Body responsible for the match, who shall take such action as is considered appropriate against the captain and bowler concerned.

8.   *Deliberate bowling of high full pitched balls*

If the umpire considers that a high full pitch which is deemed to be dangerous and unfair, as defined in 6(b) above, was deliberately bowled, then the caution and warning prescribed in 7 above shall be dispensed with. The umpire shall

(a) call and signal No ball.

(b) direct the captain, when the ball is dead, to take the bowler off forthwith.

(c) implement the remainder of the procedure as laid down in 7(c) above.

9. **Time wasting by the fielding side**

It is unfair for any member of the fielding side to waste time.

(a) If the captain of the fielding side wastes time, or allows any member of his side to waste time, or if the progress of an over is unnecessarily slow, at the first instance the umpire shall call and signal Dead ball if necessary and

(i) warn the captain, and indicate that this is a first and final warning.

(ii) inform the other umpire and the batsmen of what has occurred.

(b) If there is any further waste of time in that innings, by any member of the fielding side, the umpire shall either

(i) if the waste of time is not during the course of an over, award 5 penalty runs to the batting side. See 17 below.

Or

(ii) if the waste of time is during the course of an over, when the ball is dead, direct the captain to take the bowler off forthwith. If applicable, the over shall be completed by another bowler, who shall neither have bowled the previous over nor be allowed to bowl the next over. The bowler thus taken off shall not be allowed to bowl again in that innings.

(iii) inform the other umpire, the batsmen and, as soon as practicable, the captain of the batting side of what has occurred.

(iv) report the occurrence, with the other umpire, as soon as possible to the Executive of the fielding side and to any Governing Body responsible for the match, who shall take such action as is considered appropriate against the captain and team concerned.

10. **Batsman wasting time**

It is unfair for a batsman to waste time. In normal circumstances the striker should always be ready to take strike when the bowler is ready to start his run up.

(a) Should either batsman waste time by failing to meet this requirement, or in any other way, the following procedure shall be adopted. At the first instance, either before the bowler starts his run up or when the ball is dead, as appropriate, the umpire shall

(i) warn the batsman and indicate that this is a first and final warning. This warning shall continue to apply throughout the innings. The umpire shall so inform each incoming batsman.

(ii) inform the other umpire, the other batsman and the captain of the fielding side of what has occurred.

(iii) inform the captain of the batting side as soon as practicable.

(b) if there is any further time wasting by any batsman in that innings, the umpire shall, at the appropriate time while the ball is dead

(i) award 5 penalty runs to the fielding side. See 17 below.

(ii) inform the other umpire, the other batsman, the captain of the fielding side and, as soon as practicable, the captain of the batting side of what has occurred.

(iii) report the occurrence, with the other umpire, as soon as possible to the Executive of the batting side and to any Governing Body responsible for the match, who shall take such action as is considered appropriate against the captain and player or players and, if appropriate, the team concerned.

11.   *Damaging the pitch – area to be protected*

(a) It is incumbent on all players to avoid unnecessary damage to the pitch. It is unfair for any player to cause deliberate damage to the pitch.

(b) An area of the pitch, to be referred to as 'the protected area', is defined as that area contained within a rectangle bounded at each end by imaginary lines parallel to the popping creases and 5ft/1.52m in front of each and on the sides by imaginary lines, one each side of the imaginary line joining the centres of the two middle stumps, each parallel to it and 1ft/30.48cm from it.

12.   *Bowler running on the protected area after delivering the ball*

(a) If the bowler, after delivering the ball, runs on the protected area as defined in 11(b) above, the umpire shall at the first instance, and when the ball is dead,

    (i) caution the bowler. This caution shall continue to apply throughout the innings.

    (ii) inform the other umpire, the captain of the fielding side and the batsmen of what has occurred.

(b) If, in that innings, the same bowler runs on the protected area again after delivering the ball, the umpire shall repeat the above procedure, indicating that this is a final warning.

(c) If, in that innings, the same bowler runs on the protected area a third time after delivering the ball, when the ball is dead the umpire shall

    (i) direct the captain of the fielding side to take the bowler off forthwith. If applicable, the over shall be completed by another bowler, who shall neither have bowled the previous over nor be allowed to bowl the next over. The bowler thus taken off shall not be allowed to bowl again in that innings.

    (ii) inform the other umpire, the batsmen and, as soon as practicable, the captain of the batting side of what has occurred.

    (iii) report the occurrence, with the other umpire, as soon as possible to the Executive of the fielding side and to any Governing Body responsible for the match, who shall take such action as is considered appropriate against the captain and bowler concerned.

13. *Fielder damaging the pitch*

(a) If any fielder causes avoidable damage to the pitch, other than as in 12(a) above, at the first instance the umpire shall, when the ball is dead,

    (i) caution the captain of the fielding side, indicating that this is a first and final warning. This caution shall continue to apply throughout the innings.

    (ii) inform the other umpire and the batsmen.

(b) If there is any further avoidable damage to the pitch by any fielder in that innings, the umpire shall, when the ball is dead,

    (i) award 5 penalty runs to the batting side. See 17 below.

  (ii) inform the other umpire, the batsmen, the captain of the fielding side and, as soon as practicable, the captain of the batting side of what has occurred.

  (iii) report the occurrence, with the other umpire, as soon as possible to the Executive of the fielding side and any Governing Body responsible for the match, who shall take such action as is considered appropriate against the captain and player or players concerned.

14.   *Batsman damaging the pitch*

(a) If either batsman causes avoidable damage to the pitch, at the first instance the umpire shall, when the ball is dead,

  (i) caution the batsman. This caution shall continue to apply throughout the innings. The umpire shall so inform each incoming batsman.

  (ii) inform the other umpire, the other batsman, the captain of the fielding side and, as soon as practicable, the captain of the batting side.

(b) If there is a second instance of avoidable damage to the pitch by any batsman in that innings

  (i) the umpire shall repeat the above procedure, indicating that this is a final warning.

  (ii) additionally he shall disallow all runs to the batting side from that delivery other than the penalty for a No ball or a Wide, if applicable. The batsmen shall return to their original ends.

(c) If there is any further avoidable damage to the pitch by any batsman in that innings, the umpire shall, when the ball is dead,

  (i) disallow all runs to the batting side from that delivery other than the penalty for a No ball or a Wide, if applicable.

  (ii) additionally award 5 penalty runs to the fielding side. See 17 below.

  (iii) inform the other umpire, the other batsman, the captain of the fielding side and, as soon as practicable, the captain of the batting side of what has occurred.

  (iv) report the occurrence, with the other umpire, as soon as possible to the Executive of the batting side and any Governing Body responsible for the match, who shall take such action as is considered appropriate against the captain and player or players concerned.

15.   *Bowler attempting to run out non-striker before delivery*
The bowler is permitted, before entering his delivery stride, to attempt to run out the non-striker. The ball shall not count in the over.

The umpire shall call and signal Dead ball as soon as possible if the bowler fails in the attempt to run out the non-striker.

16.   *Batsmen stealing a run*
It is unfair for the batsmen to attempt to steal a run during the bowler's run up. Unless the bowler attempts to run out either batsman – see 15 above and Law 24.4 (Bowler throwing towards striker's end before delivery) – the umpire shall

(i) call and signal Dead ball as soon as the batsmen cross in any such attempt.

(ii) return the batsmen to their original ends.

(iii) award 5 penalty runs to the fielding side. See 17 below.

(iv) inform the other umpire, the batsmen, the captain of the fielding side and, as soon as practicable, the captain of the batting side of the reason for the action taken.

(v) report the occurrence, with the other umpire, as soon as possible to the Executive of the batting side and any Governing Body responsible for the match, who shall take such action as is considered appropriate against the captain and player or players concerned.

17.   *Penalty runs*
(a) When penalty runs are awarded to either side, when the ball is dead the umpire shall signal the penalty runs to the scorers as laid down in Law 3.14 (Signals).

(b) Notwithstanding any provisions elsewhere in the Laws, penalty runs shall not be awarded once the match is concluded as defined in Law 16.9 (Conclusion of a match).

(c) When 5 penalty runs are awarded to the batting side, under either Law 2.6 (Player returning without permission) or Law 41 (The fielder) or under 3, 4, 5, 9 or 13 above, then

    (i) they shall be scored as penalty extras and shall be in addition to any other penalties.

    (ii) they shall not be regarded as runs scored from either the immediately preceding delivery or the following delivery, and shall be in addition to any runs from those deliveries.

    (iii) the batsmen shall not change ends solely by reason of the 5 run penalty.

(d) When 5 penalty runs are awarded to the fielding side, under Law 18.5(b) (Deliberate short runs), or under 10, 14 or 16 above, they shall be added as penalty extras to that side's total of runs in its most recently completed innings. If the fielding side has not completed an innings, the 5 penalty extras shall be added to its next innings.

18. *Players' conduct*

If there is any breach of the Spirit of the Game by a player failing to comply with the instructions of an umpire, or criticising his decisions by word or action, or showing dissent, or generally behaving in a manner which might bring the game into disrepute, the umpire concerned shall immediately report the matter to the other umpire. The umpires together shall

    (i) inform the player's captain of the occurrence, instructing the latter to take action.

    (ii) warn him of the gravity of the offence, and tell him that it will be reported to higher authority.

    (iii) report the occurrence as soon as possible to the Executive of the player's team and any Governing Body responsible for the match, who shall take such action as is considered appropriate against the captain and player or players, and, if appropriate, the team concerned.

Appendix A

Law 8 (The Wickets)

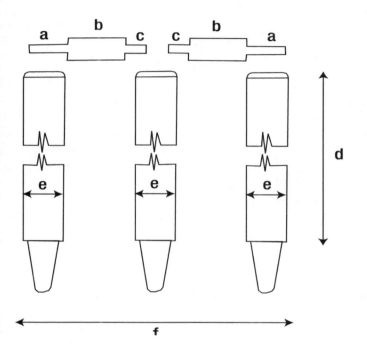

	Bails	
	Senior	**Junior**
Overall	4 5/16 in / 10.95 cm	3 13/16 in / 9.68 cm
a=	1 3/8 in / 3.49 cm	1 1/4 in / 3.18 cm
b=	2 1/8 in / 5.40 cm	1 13/16 in / 4.60 cm
c=	1 3/16 in / 2.06 cm	3/4 in / 1.91 cm

	Stumps	
	Senior	**Junior**
Height (d)	28 in / 71.1 cm	27 in / 68.58 cm
Diameter (e)		
max.	1 1/2 in / 3.81 cm	1 3/8 in / 3.49 cm
min.	1 3/8 in / 3.49 cm	1 1/4 in / 3.18 cm

	Overall	
Width of wicket (f)	9 in / 22.86 cm	8 in / 20.32 cm

Appendix B

Laws 7 (The Pitch) and 9 (The Bowling, Popping and Return Creases)

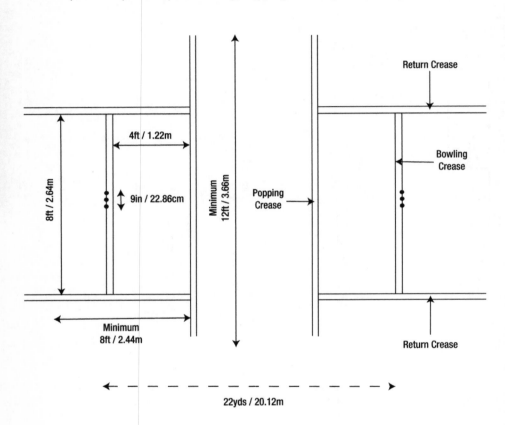

Appendix C

Law 40.2 Gloves

These diagrams show what is meant by:
- no webbing between fingers
- single piece of flat non-stretch material between index finger and thumb solely as a means of support
- not forming a pouch when hand is extended

Appendix D

Definitions and explanations of words or phrases not defined in the text

The Toss is the toss for choice of innings.

Before the toss is at any time before the toss on the day the match is expected to start or, in the case of a one day match, on the day that match is due to take place. Before the match is at any time before the toss, not restricted to the day on which the toss is to take place.

During the match is at any time after the toss until the conclusion of the match, whether play is in progress or not.

Implements of the game are the bat, the ball, the stumps and bails.

The field of play is the area contained within the boundary edge.

The square is a specially prepared area of the field of play within which the match pitch is situated.

Inside edge is the edge on the same side as the nearer wicket.

Behind in relation to stumps and creases, is on the side further from the stumps and creases at the other end of the pitch. Conversely, in front of is on the side nearer to the stumps and creases at the other end of the pitch.

A batsman's ground – at each end of the pitch, the whole area of the field of play behind the popping crease is the ground at that end for a batsman.

In front of the line of the striker's wicket is in the area of the field of play in front of the imaginary line joining the fronts of the stumps at one end; this line to be considered extended in both directions to the boundary.

Behind the wicket is in the area of the field of play behind the imaginary line joining the backs of the stumps at one end; this line to be considered extended in both directions to the boundary.

Behind the wicket-keeper is behind the wicket at the striker's end, as defined above, but in line with both sets of stumps, and further from the stumps than the wicketkeeper.

Off side/on side – see diagram below.

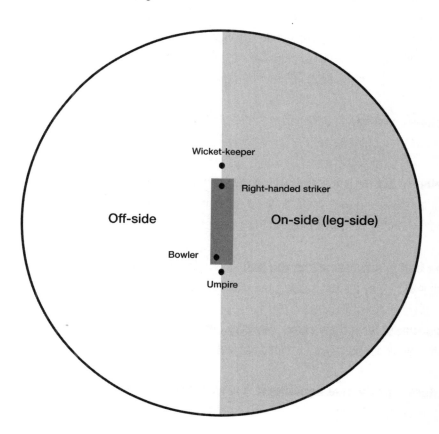

Umpire – where the word 'umpire' is used on its own, it always means 'the umpire at the bowler's end', though this full description is sometimes used for emphasis or clarity. Otherwise, the phrases **the umpire concerned**, **the umpire at the striker's end**, **either umpire** indicate which umpire is intended.

Umpires together agree applies to decisions which the umpires are to make jointly, independently of the players.

Fielder is any one of those 11 or fewer players currently on the field of play who together compose the fielding side. This definition includes not only both the bowler and the wicket-keeper but also any legitimate substitute fielding instead of a nominated player. It excludes any nominated player absent from the field of play, or who has been absent from the field of play and who has not obtained the umpire's permission to return.

A player going briefly outside the boundary in the course of discharging his duties as a fielder is not absent from the field of play nor, for the purposes of Law 2.5 (Fielder absent or leaving the field), is he to be regarded as having left the field of play.

Delivery swing is the motion of the bowler's arm during which normally he releases the ball for a delivery.

Delivery stride is the stride during which the delivery swing is made, whether the ball is released or not. It starts when the bowler's back foot lands for that stride and ends when the front foot lands in the same stride.

The ball is struck/strikes the ball unless specifically defined otherwise, mean 'the ball is struck by the bat'/'strikes the ball with the bat'.

Rebounds directly/strikes directly and similar phrases mean without contact with any fielder but do not exclude contact with the ground.

External protective equipment is any visible item of apparel worn for protection against external blows.

For a batsman, items permitted are a helmet, external leg guards (batting pads), batting gloves and, if visible, fore-arm guards.

For a fielder, only a helmet is permitted, except in the case of a wicket-keeper, for whom wicket-keeping pads and gloves are also permitted.

Clothing – anything that a player is wearing that is not classed as external protective equipment, including such items as spectacles or jewellery, is classed as clothing, even though he may be wearing some items of apparel, which are not visible, for protection. A bat being carried by a batsman does not come within this definition of clothing.

The bat – the following are to be considered as part of the bat
- the whole of the bat itself.
- the whole of a glove (or gloves) worn on a hand (or hands) holding the bat.
- the hand (or hands) holding the bat, if the batsman is not wearing a glove on that hand or on those hands.

Equipment – a batsman's equipment is his bat, as defined above, together with any external protective equipment that he is wearing.
A fielder's equipment is any external protective equipment that he is wearing.

Person – a player's person is his physical person (flesh and blood) together with any clothing or legitimate external protective equipment that he is wearing except, in the case of a batsman, his bat.

A hand, whether gloved or not, that is not holding the bat is part of the batsman's person.

No item of clothing or equipment is part of the player's person unless it is attached to him.

For a batsman, a glove being held but not worn is part of his person.

For a fielder, an item of clothing or equipment he is holding in his hand or hands is not part of his person.